David H Maxfield

DOES IT REALLY MATTER WHAT I BELIEVE ABOUT GOD?

A comparison of world religions and beliefs to help you make your decision.

What if it matters to God what you believe?
Eternity is a long time to regret making the wrong choice

Copyright @2021 by David H Maxfield

All rights reserved. No part of this book may be reproduced in any form or by any electronic or mechanical means, including information storage and retrieval systems, without permission in writing from the publisher, except by reviewers, who may quote brief passages in a review.

This publication contains the opinions and ideas of its author. It is intended to provide helpful and informative material on the subjects addressed in the publication. The author and publisher specifically disclaim all responsibility for any liability, loss or risk, personal or otherwise, which is incurred as a consequence, directly or indirectly, of the use and application of any of the contents of this book.

WORKBOOK PRESS LLC
187 E Warm Springs Rd,
Suite B285, Las Vegas, NV 89119, USA

Website: https://workbookpress.com/
Hotline: 1-888-818-4856
Email: admin@workbookpress.com

Ordering Information:
Quantity sales. Special discounts are available on quantity purchases by corporations, associations, and others.
For details, contact the publisher at the address above.

ISBN-13:   978-1-956017-15-1 (Paperback Version)
            978-1-956017-16-8 (Digital Version)

REV. DATE: 23/07/2021

Does it really matter what I believe about God?

David H. Maxfield

New International Version, "NIV"
King James Version, "KJV"
New King James Version, "NKJV"
American Standard Version, "ASV"
New American Standard, "NAS"
Contemporary English Version, "CEV"
The Living Bible, "TLB"

Contents

Preface ·10

Introduction ·12

Does it really matter what I believe about God? · · · · · · · · · · · · · · ·14

Where are you in relationship to God? ·20

Obviously, all paths do not lead to God ·20

Section I · 29

    "Monotheists," those believing in one God · · · · · · · · · · · · · · · · 29

    Judaism ·36

    Roman Catholicism ·53

    Islam · 75

    Jehovah's Witnesses · 93

Section II · 107

    "Polytheists," those that believe in many Gods · · · · · · · · · · · · · · 107

    Mormonism · 108

    Hinduism · 133

Section III · 141

    Those "Believing they are God or can become Godlike" · · · · · · · · 141

Christian Science 143

Church of Scientology 148

Shinto 152

Other Beliefs 155

Section IV 162

Worshiping Satan 162

Section V 162

"Atheists" deny that God exists 171

Section VI 181

"Agnostics," don't know or don't care if God exists 181

Buddhism 185

Confucianism 199

Section VII 209

Those seeking to know God 209

Section VIII 240

Knowing and worshiping God 240

Understanding the Trinity 243

Understanding our relationship to God 263

God will judge us 270

Understanding the relationship we can have with God 278

Decision time 290

After our decision, what's next? · 297

Living a life, that God rewards · 315

The Great Commission · 319

Resources · 321

Appendix A · 323

The prophecies fulfilled in Jesus, the last days of his life

Preface

The purpose of this book is to help you understand God, your relationship to God, and why it does matter to God, what you believe.

The book is divided into sections, then chapters. The sections correspond to the chart in the introduction under "Where are you in relationship to God?" The chapters are either about a specific religion or belief system like Judaism, Islam, Hinduism, etc., or they may be about a subgroup. For example, Christianity is a belief. Under that general heading there are many religious groups identifying themselves as "Christians." Often, they agree on basic principles, but there are subgroups with significant differences. As we shall see, there are major differences between what Catholics, Protestants, Jehovah's Witnesses and Mormons believe.

Sometimes a religious group could fall into multiple categories. For example, Mormons identify themselves with Jesus Christ, but unlike others claiming to be Christian, they are *polytheistic,* believing in many Gods. In addition to that, their ultimate goal is *exaltation,* to achieve Godhood. This should not be confused with others who believe they are either emanations from God, or that one day they will reach a point of becoming one with God, *monism.* For Mormons, their goal is to become a God, just like God the Father, their creator.

Others like Hinduism and Buddhism have some common beliefs like karma and reincarnation, but they are exact opposites when it comes to God. Hindus are polytheistic while Buddhists are seeking a state of enlightenment, *nirvana,* where ego is extinguished. Buddhists believe that ultimate reality is an impersonal void or emptiness.

Then again, Buddhists like Christians, Jews, Muslims, and more, can be broken into at least two or more subgroups. Therefore, it is more important to try to look at one's beliefs rather than some label, which is why this book is broken down by section.

Introduction

My purpose in writing this book is to help people make an informed decision about the most important question of their life. "Does it Really Matter What I Believe About God?"

My standard is to seek and share information obtained from sources that I believe to be reliable. My guideline, "When in doubt, leave it out."

My method is to quote whenever possible, and to interject my observations based on my overall studies and experiences.

My measurement is to be truthful. The fact of the matter is that God will hold anyone assuming the role that I have to a higher standard. I do not take this lightly. I usually quote passages at length and with commentary so as not to take things out of context. Otherwise, the meaning can be distorted and people can be misled. I believe this is the main reason for so many differing beliefs and divisions between people who claim they believe the Bible to be the word of God.

For your convenience, I have included selected passages from the Bible in this book. Moreover, my hope is that many people who might read this may not have a Bible yet. I have taken the liberty to include passages from different translations, drawing heavily from the New International Version, "NIV." This is not an endorsement, but I have read several versions, and I just think it provides a good balance, being both accurate and easy to understand.

There are several reliable versions where the translators were able to refer to the original manuscripts. For example, many people adhere to the King James Version, "KJV." It is very poetic, but just not as easy to understand as others written in the language of today. The New American Standard, "NAS" is a more literal translation to English from the original Hebrew and Greek, but, in my opinion, does not seem to flow as well. The Living Bible, "TLB," is not translated word for word, but gives us a rendering that is meant to convey the original meaning in terms we can easily understand. The goal of the translators for the Contemporary English Version, "CEV," was to create a work that was easy to comprehend by the listener when someone reads it to them.

My suggestion is that whatever version you prefer, you make the decision to have an open mind. Read from it rather than reading into it something that is not there. This can take the form of circular reasoning; starting with the conclusion, then examining the evidence and distorting the facts to validate it.

For example, someone who believes the world is flat sees only the horizon, because this seems to validate his or her belief. If shown a picture of the earth from space, they would challenge the authenticity and raise doubts about why it appears to be round. They could blame the camera equipment, that something caused distortions, or that someone is trying to fool them. Then they might question the motives of the person who showed it to them. Finally, in an attempt to cling to their original belief, they just choose to ignore the picture and forget they have ever seen it. While the illustration may sound silly, this is just an example of the routine that people do every day.

After deciding to have an open mind and being willing to learn, there is something else. To gain a better understanding of a passage, always read it in context with the verses preceding and following. Then look at the chapter as a whole. What is the theme? Consider the chapter in the context of the book.

Then, who was the author? Who were they writing to, and what were the circumstances? Finally, consider it from the perspective of the entire message of the Bible.

My hope is that this book unites people in their basic beliefs and demonstrates that it is important to God what you believe.

Throughout history, people have asked themselves:

Does God exist?

If so, what is God like?

Is there more than one God?

What do I want from God?

What does God expect from me?

"Does it really matter what I believe about God?"

The answer depends on whether or not God exists. If not, it really does not matter much what you believe. On the other hand, if there is a God, maybe the question should be rephrased. Does it matter to God what I believe?

If it matters to God, what you believe may affect you during your lifetime, and beyond. Eternity is a long time to regret making the wrong decisions. You need to decide before it is too late. Let us face it; any of us could die from an illness or injury at any time. None of us know how many heartbeats we get.

The purpose of this book is to help you understand God, your relationship to God, and why it does matter to God, what you believe.

It is no wonder that people are confused.

We have so many mixed messages:

How many times have you heard statements made by people that have strong opinions about God that seem contradictory? For example:

"There must be a supreme being, just look at the creation!"

"Hasn't science proven the theory of evolution?"

"Aren't all the varieties of plants and animals the result of millions of years of evolution?"

What about the possibility of intelligent design that many scholars and scientists believe?

"God is merciful. He loves and cares about us."

"God is just. He judges and will punish us when we disobey."

"People trying to please God are kind to other people."

"People wage war and kill people in the name of God."

"You receive your rewards in heaven."

"There is no heaven. Your rewards are the joy, if any, from the fame, fortune, and power you attain while you are alive."

"We can have a personal relationship with God, who hears and answers our prayers."

"God is unapproachable. We can never know God."

"After we die, God judges us."

"After we die, we are reincarnated. The process goes on until we attain perfection."

Alternatively, others believe that after we die, we continue in our progression to become just like God.

"There is one God."

"There are many Gods."

There are so many religions or belief systems.

"Judaism, Christianity, Islam - what's the difference between Moses, Jesus and Muhammad?"

"Hinduism, Buddhism, Confucianism, etc. - aren't they all pretty much the same?"

"Aren't the Torah, Bible, Quran, and the words of Confucius, Buddha, and all the others called scripture? How can you know what to believe?"

Further divisions and variations.

Over the years, many of these groups split into subgroups. For example, Judaism can be further divided into Orthodox, Conservative and Reformed.

Christianity has Roman Catholics, who have a pope as their

spiritual leader and Eastern Orthodox, who do not. Yet, both claim an unbroken apostolic succession from the time of Christ to the present day. Both add tradition to the Bible in contrast to Protestantism, which generally relies upon the Bible as the sole authority. Protestants may or may not follow a central church authority or hierarchy. Then there are Christians who distinguish themselves as neither Catholic nor Protestant. Some have a central governing body, and some claim the Bible as their only authority.

This is somewhat like Islam. One group, the Sunnis, emphasize the authority of their written scriptures. On the other hand, their *Imam*, or spiritual leader, influences the Shiites more.

There were also splits in other beliefs. Buddhism, for example, has two major groups, Theravada, and Mahayana.

With only these few examples, we can see that just because someone identifies themselves with a certain group, it does not mean we know much about what they really believe. Sometimes these splits occur over major issues and sometimes over minor ones.

I know of a large Christian church that first split over whether to have a central authority or not. Then they split again over whether to have piano music at worship service. The central authority versus local control is easier to understand. However, it makes you wonder why they would split over a piano? You have to look a little deeper for the answer. The group that did not want the piano was convinced that the New Testament of the Bible, in effect, replaced the Old Testament. Therefore, unless it was mentioned in the New Testament you should not do it. The group they split with pointed out that the Old Testament was often quoted in the New Testament so they felt that both are valid. Music and even dancing were included in the Old Testament, and if it was used in worship then, it should be now. However, the dancing was not comparable to the dancing one might think of by today's standards.

I once had the pleasure to attend a worship service at a congregation of Messianic Jews. The service was probably conducted much in the same way it would have been 2,000 years ago. There was a time for greetings, prayer, teaching, singing, and dancing. The dancing was done in a circle and it was done as a form of worship for God. The entire service was beautiful and fitting for this group of Jews that believe Jesus is the Messiah.

So why was there a problem with the piano? One group was being very legalistic in attempting to do what they believe God wanted. The other, who actually believed much the same as the first, took a more liberal view of worship. It reminds me of the story about two lawyers who attended two different schools of law. If you asked the first whether you should do something or not, his reply would be, "Unless the law says you can do it, you had better not." However, when you asked the other attorney the same question, his reply was, "Unless the law says you can't do something, go ahead and do it."

Transformations and unions, or blended faiths.

The opposite of division, unions are formed when some beliefs are adopted by a different religion. For example, Hinduism influenced Buddhism, and Buddhism influenced Confucianism.

Then again, you would hardly recognize Hinduism today, if comparing it to the original set of beliefs. Over the past 3,500 years or so, it has had an effect on a number of other belief systems. At the same time, Hinduism itself has been influenced by others and has evolved into a combination of beliefs. So much, that now rather than differentiating themselves, they say that all paths lead to God.

I suppose it is impractical to believe that everyone will agree all the time, on every issue. The downside is, sometimes people compromise when they should not. If you have the truth, why compromise? Why settle for less than the truth? The simple reason people compromise is that it avoids confrontation. Therefore, the recent concepts of "relative morality," and that "there is no absolute truth," are being taught in our public education systems, and accepted by the people of the last couple of generations.

What about when two groups, within a certain belief, disagree and each one believes so strongly that compromise is out of the question? My suggestion is that all concerned seek the truth. Check your information. Is it accurate? What has influenced you? Are there any preconceived notions or prejudices that may be affecting you? Recognize the fundamental truth and do not compromise on the essentials, but do not be as concerned about the non-essentials.

Many more religions and more contradictory messages could be listed. The point is that labels do not mean much. It is what you believe that matters.

Where are you in relationship to God?

Chart with eight segments:
- Know and worship God
- Seek to know God
- Unsure or don't care if God exists
- Deny that God Exists
- Worship Satan
- Believe they are God or can become like God
- Believe in many Gods
- Believe in one God

Everyone who has ever lived will be able to find themselves somewhere on the chart.

Obviously, all paths do not lead to God.

As the chart illustrates, all paths do not lead to God. What you believe does matter. Therefore, a careful examination of why you believe what you believe is important.

At this point, you may want to turn to the section or sections that seem most relevant to you. If you do, that is fine. However, I would encourage you to read the entire book to gain a better understanding of what others believe. Additionally, each section contains lessons from scripture that will give you a deeper understanding of who God is and the relationship God wants with you.

What factors have had an influence on you?

When or where you were born.

Interestingly, a recent survey provides evidence that where you were born may have an influence on you. When people in the United States were asked about their perception of God, there were predominant views according to region. Those in the Northeast responded that God was judgmental, in the Midwest they thought God was benevolent, while those in the Southern regions thought God was active in their lives, those in the West more often concluded that God was distant, unknowable, or unapproachable.

As another example, if you had been born around 1500 BC, Hinduism or Judaism would likely have had an influence on you. Then within about 100 years, from 660 to 550 BC, new beliefs like Shinto, Taoism, Buddhism and Confucianism all arrived on the scene. Following these were Christianity, 30AD and Islam around 622 AD.

History reveals that what was once a pure religious belief was polluted or diluted by multiple beliefs converging together so that you can hardly recognize the original. From my studies, that disturbs God. He wants a personal relationship with us. He is jealous. He wants us to know Him as he knows us and have a one-on-one relationship. This topic is explored more later on in this book.

The ability to exchange ideas.

Less than 100 years ago, the primary means of travel was a horse, train, or ship. We were landlocked. Years ago, many people grew up in small communities. They were not as exposed to different religions or ideologies because of a lack of communications. I was born more than a half century ago. I remember visiting my aunt who lived in a small farming community. She still had a crank telephone and a party line. Now we find ourselves truly in the information age with little or no barriers. Anyone with access to a television with satellite reception can see the news as it happens, anywhere in the world. People connected to the internet have access to a global knowledge pool with just a few keystrokes.

However, just because these forms of communication are readily available to some does not mean they are available to everyone. Some countries still restrict access and censor information. Other countries may be more open but are still developing.

Therefore, when and where you were born could have an effect on what you believe. In addition to that, people do not always talk about their beliefs very much. For many, social etiquette dictates that we avoid the subjects of religion and politics in order to avoid arguments.

I think that is unfortunate. Like most people, I myself want to avoid arguments, but I do enjoy good discussions. Not debates, which are just controlled arguments. I am talking about an open exchange of ideas where people are seeking the truth. That does not mean they will always agree. It just means they will give each other a fair hearing.

The region of the world.

Diverse cultures separated by natural barriers have come up with different ideas about God, or Gods and Goddesses. Many people simply accept the prominent belief of the region. They do not even question it.

Throughout history, the leaders of some countries have designated a certain belief as their official religion. Some examples are Japan, where at one time Christianity was banned while Buddhism was made a branch of the state. Later, it removed the ban on Christianity, and demoted Buddhism and made Shinto the official religion.

During the period of Marxism, the concept of God, and any religious practice was suppressed. Karl Marx declared himself an atheist and taught that there is no creator and after death, we just cease to exist. Other Marxist, communist states have also opposed religion, unless it would be in their best interest to allow it.

Today, it appears that the leaders of China do not mind that Marxism is on the way out and there is a resurgence of Confucianism to fill the void. It seems the people have been starving for something more meaningful in their life. Confucianism promotes a strong work ethic, commitment to families, loyalty, and respect. Therefore, to the leaders of China, it might seem that communism and Confucianism do mix because it works for them.

If not state sponsored, it might be a cultural thing. You will find places where everybody dresses in their best clothes, and attends a place of worship, religiously once a week. That is not to say they are "religious," rather that it is just expected. Maybe it would be better described as a "tradition or obligation." On the other hand, some cultures are best described as God-less.

What your parents believed.

How much of an influence did your parents have on you? Were they "religious?" If you grew up just accepting their religion, you might want to question it. Was there prayer in your home? Did your parents attend a place of worship regularly? Maybe they did not attend but they identified themselves with a certain religion or group. Did they give you a mixed message? Do as I say, not as I do; making sure you attended services, but never going themselves.

Alternatively, did you come from a mixed marriage? Maybe your father and mother had different beliefs? On the other hand, maybe you did not have exposure to any religious beliefs at all.

What experiences you have had with religion.

I know a great many people who were brought up in one religion or another but drifted away. Sometimes they just found other things they would rather do than attending church. Others became disillusioned with what they had been taught and disassociate themselves with any organized religion. Typically, they believe in God, but are unsure about heaven or hell, preferring to ignore judgment.

What you were taught in school.

Your schoolteachers probably have, or had, a great influence on you. Just think about how much time you spend, or have spent, in a classroom compared to the rest of your day. In their position, they have the power to mold your thoughts at a time in your life when you are most impressionable.

On the subject of world history, you may have been taught about several belief systems. Frankly, there have been many wars fought in the name of God. Even today, there are conflicts where everyone would like to believe God is on their side.

What else has influenced you?

We are constantly bombarded with messages. Sometimes they are obvious, like commercials, which attempt to get us to buy something. Other times the message is subtle; trying to get us to buy into something like an idea or belief. Television, movies, music, books, and even video games can have an effect on us. Current events and social issues like "Pro Choice vs. Pro Life" debates tend to polarize us. Peer pressure should never be underestimated. Almost everyone wants to fit in and be accepted, sometimes at the expense of good judgment.

The point is that it may be wise for you to think about what has had an influence on you. As the expression goes, "garbage in, garbage out." While this was coined for the computer age, it applies to us too. If our minds are like sponges, you should consider what you are soaking up. Otherwise, you could end up with stinking thinking.

Where you are might be as a result of your indecision.

Sometimes people seek to have a relationship with God, and sometimes they decide to separate themselves. Others just do not think about it that much.

Are you in your comfort zone?

Maybe you think religion is okay for others, but you do not think you need it?

Alternatively, you might be cruising through life and have not given it much thought. Sometimes we need to be outside our comfort zones to consider any relationship with God.

The following chart illustrates how we react to living within our comfort zone. While moving in it, we seem to function normally. Once outside, we tend to do things that move us back into our comfort zone. You might have heard about people who came into a lot of money, only to lose it a short time later. For example, there have been studies of people who won the lottery. Within a few years, they were back in the same position as before they won. On the other hand, people who find themselves below their comfort zone will often dig deeper, work harder, or do whatever it takes to move them back up to an acceptable level.

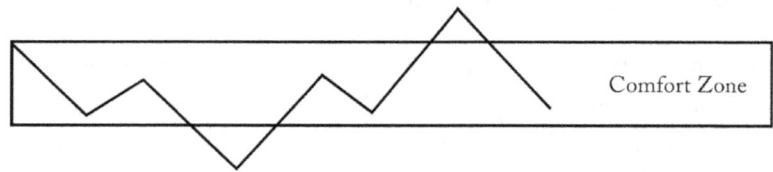

It is when we are outside our comfort zone that we probably think more about our relationship with God. Sometimes people are so low that they finally plea to God to help them. On the other hand, sometimes people achieve so much they despair, wondering if that is all life is about.

Deion Sanders wrote a book called *Chasing the Wind* about himself and his life changing experience. As a premier baseball and football player, he earned both fame and fortune. Yet, at one point he wanted to commit suicide. He apparently went outside his comfort zone at both ends. Sometimes that is what it takes for God to get our attention.

Were you ever angry with God?

Sometimes that happens when people are hurt or disappointed. They cannot understand why a God who is supposed to be good lets bad things happen. However, that assumes that God is controlling everything. Whether or not God can control everything is not the issue. Throughout history there have been many miracles recorded. By one definition:

> *Miracles: Historic events or natural phenomena that appear to violate natural laws (from Nelson's Illustrated Bible Dictionary, Copyright (c)1986, Thomas Nelson Publishers)*

Sometimes God, according to His purpose, may choose to

get involved. Other times He may choose to do nothing, and just let nature take its course. After all, He created what we refer to as nature. That does not mean God does not care about us. This will be discussed in detail in the section about God.

Are you confused?

Maybe you have been seeking a relationship with God, but you are simply confused. Good news. This book is for you.

Are you afraid of making a commitment?

Are you afraid of failure? That once making a decision about God that you will not be able to keep your commitment. I have good news for you that we will discuss later in this book.

Do you want to wait until you have cleaned up your life?

There is good news and bad news. The bad news is that will never totally happen as long as you live. The good news is that is not what God requires.

Are you so bad that you think God will never forgive you?

Good news, God will accept you on certain conditions regardless of how you have lived your life.

Do you think that you are so good that you know God will accept you?

Bad news. You are kidding yourself. We all fall short of God's standards.

Are you too busy?

Your decision is too important to put off until you get around to it. It has eternal consequences. Please, do not put it off until it is too late.

What if tomorrow never comes?

People are dying every day of injuries or illness, and it does not matter what their age is. Nobody knows how many heartbeats they will get. Maybe, *just maybe*, that is the point. What if it does matter to God what you believe, and He cares more about how you live your life than how long you live. What if there is not a second chance? As we read in the Bible:

Heb 9:27

27 Just as man is destined to die once, and after that to face judgment, "NIV"

Maybe God would like you to understand that and make your choice before it is too late. If none of us know how long we will live, then maybe we need to make a decision sooner rather than later.

It is your choice.

When given a choice, you either accept or reject. Not accepting an invitation is equal to rejecting it. Rejecting God is a decision that has eternal consequences. It is not just about here; it is about hereafter.

Section I
Monotheists, those believing in one God.

Monotheists believe in one God who is a separate entity. He is not part of His creation. As the Creator, He is all-powerful. He has passions like anger and love. They fear and revere Him because He is both just and merciful. They seek to know Him and submit to His will. In effect, they worship Him.

Three major religious groups in this section, Jews, Christians, and Muslims, share some beliefs. These history-based religions make up more than 50% of the world's population.

Judaism

What is confusing for some is that just because one identifies them self as Jewish, does not mean they practice Judaism. Rather, they may only be identifying themselves as Jews by nationality. Those practicing Judaism can be further broken down into subgroups, among them: Orthodox, Conservative, and Reform. Their basic beliefs are that Moses probably wrote the first five books of the Bible, which are also known as the *Pentateuch*.

They believe there is one God, the God of Abraham, who is their patriarch. They believe in a *Messiah*, being translated as the *Anointed* one, who will take away the sins of mankind. They also believe in a Messiah, who will establish His kingdom on earth. Early Jewish scholars thought this could either be two Messiahs or one Messiah who comes twice.

Christianity

Christians believe as Jews do with a couple of exceptions.

Christians believe in a larger collection of writings known as the Old Testament, which includes the Pentateuch, and the New Testament.

With regard to one God, Jesus quoted Deut 6:4, from the Pentateuch, in the gospel of Mark. When asked, "Of all the commandments, which is the most important?"

> *Mark 12:29-31*
>
> *29 "The most important one," answered Jesus, "is this: 'Hear, O Israel, the Lord our God, the Lord is one. 30 Love the Lord your God with all your heart and with all your soul and with all your mind and with all your strength.'*

Yet, Jesus is probably quoted more often from verse 31.

> *31 The second is this: 'Love your neighbor as yourself.' There is no commandment greater than these." "NIV"*

To clarify a misconception, Christians do not believe that the *Trinity* means there are three Gods. Obviously, as they believe the words of Jesus, they believe in one God, but that God has manifested himself in three persons, the Father, Son, and Holy Spirit. There is more on the Trinity contained later in this book.

For further clarification, the word *Christian* means a follower of Christ. *Christ* is from the Greek, "Christos," which is the Greek version of "Messiah" in Hebrew, being translated as the "Anointed."

Christians believe that Jesus fulfilled the first purpose of atoning for our sins, when he was put to death. They believe that Jesus, who was sinless, died to satisfy the requirements of the law for people who were sinful. Like a scapegoat, one person paid the price for many that were guilty. *Scapegoa*t is a term you may be familiar with, but for further clarification, be sure to read the chapter on Judaism.

Christians believe that after Jesus died, he was resurrected, and that he will return and at that time establish his kingdom.

Islam

Muslims believe a variation on what Jews and Christians believe.

Fundamentally, they believe that there are many prophets of God, the last, and the greatest of which was Muhammad. They believe the first five books of the Bible as written by Moses, Psalms written by David, and the Gospels about Jesus.

In addition to that, they believe the angel Gabriel was instrumental in revealing the Quran, further revelations from God to Muhammad.

United by a common patriarch.

While these groups often seem to be at odds with one another, they all share the belief that God revealed Himself to the world through the same person, Abraham. That Abraham was to offer his son as a sacrifice to God, and at the last minute, the LORD interceded.

Gen 22:10-14

> *10 Then he reached out his hand and took the knife to slay his son. 11 But the angel of the LORD called out to him from heaven, "Abraham! Abraham!"*

"Here I am," he replied.

12 "Do not lay a hand on the boy," he said. "Do not do anything to him. Now I know that you fear God, because you have not withheld from me your son, your only son."

13 Abraham looked up and there in a thicket he saw a ram caught by its horns. He went over and took the ram and sacrificed it as a burnt offering instead of his son. 14 So Abraham called that place The LORD Will Provide. "NIV"

Divided by two sons.

God promised Abraham a son through his wife Sarai. (Her name was later changed to Sarah, as Abraham was changed from Abram). Since they were both advanced in years, and Sarai had not become pregnant, she thought she might help God.

Gen 16:1-2

16:1 Now Sarai, Abram's wife, had borne him no children. But she had an Egyptian maidservant named Hagar; 2 so she said to Abram, "The LORD has kept me from having children. Go, sleep with my maidservant; perhaps I can build a family through her." "NIV"

Hagar did conceive and her son was named Ishmael, and later Sarai conceived and bore a son named Isaac. Muslims and Jews disagree which son was to be offered to God by Abraham, and through whose descendants God was to bless the world.

While Jews and Muslims contest the genealogy, Christians see the significance in *"The LORD Will Provide."* Substitute sacrifices were made to atone for sins. More on this is scattered throughout this book, as it is the main point of the Bible.

How reliable is the Bible?

Since all of these major groups believe in the Bible, we should question how reliable it is. There have been many good books on this subject. The unique nature of our Bible helps prove its divine source as Josh McDowell explains.

▶ Written over 1500 years.

▶ Written by more than 40 authors: Peasants, kings, military leaders, philosophers, fisherman, tax collectors, poets, musicians, shepherds, former Jesus' haters.

▶ Written in different places, from a prison cell to a palace.

▶ Written on three continents.

▶ Written in three languages, Hebrew, Aramaic, and Greek.

▶ Many different topics such as: Marriage, Divorce, Government, Lawsuits, Employers, Sex, Parenting, Conflict resolution, Diet, and Holy Living.

▶ Only one person is the focus in the Bible—Jesus Christ.

The Old Testament teaches us about the need for a Savior, and how we can recognize him. The New Testament, through prophecy fulfilled, shows us who our Savior is, and how he wants us to live our lives.

From Tim LaHaye's book, *Bible Prophecy, What You Need to Know*, published by Harvest House, "The Bible is not a single book, but a library of books containing almost one-third prophetic writings. Moses, Samuel, Daniel, Isaiah, Paul, and other lesser-known prophets wrote much of the 66 volumes.

There are 16 books on prophecy in the Old Testament, and 4 books in the New Testament. Just from the amount of material covered in Scripture called prophecy, it is clear that God intended for His children to study it."

The Bible contains Psalms, which are written to music, as worship, praise, and requests to God. The Bible also contains a collection of proverbs, or wisdom writings, for guidance in living our lives. These in themselves could be compared to the writings of others, but to me the best evidence for the validity of the Bible is prophecy fulfilled.

Nothing compares to the Bible when it comes to prophecy fulfilled.

In his book, *The Case for Christ,* Zondervan Publishing House, Lee Strobel details his personal investigation of the evidence for Jesus. He describes himself as a former spiritual skeptic, bordering on atheism, nearly denying that God exists. Through his experience as an investigative journalist, with a legal background, he spent twenty-one months studying various resources before drawing his conclusions. It makes for remarkably interesting reading, but for me the strongest evidence is through prophecies fulfilled.

In one chapter he considers the odds that these were just coincidences. What are the odds of eight prophecies being fulfilled in one person, Jesus? Someone calculated, one in one hundred million billion. That number is millions of times greater than the total number who have ever walked on this planet. As an illustration, you would have enough silver dollars to cover the state of Texas to a depth of two feet. Then you could mark one of the dollars and hide it in the stack. Then have a blindfolded person wander the state, reach down, and pick the marked coin on their first attempt.

As though that were not enough, there were actually forty-eight messianic prophecies fulfilled. Mathematician Peter W. Stoner computes that probability at one chance in a trillion, trillion, trillion, trillion, trillion, trillion, trillion, trillion, trillion, trillion, trillion, trillion, trillion. Our minds cannot comprehend a number that big. What we can conclude is that we can trust who Jesus is and that the Bible is reliable.

Judaism

Introduction

It is difficult to estimate the number of Jews today because the answer is complex. People can be Jewish by birth, as a nationality, yet not practice Judaism. Then there are divisions within Judaism across a broad spectrum of beliefs for those identifying themselves as Orthodox, Conservative or Reformed.

The Bible describes the descendants of Abraham as the chosen ones. What is less clear is why they are described this way. What were they chosen for? Being chosen, does that mean that they are superior to others? Does it mean that God loves them more? Does He admit them to heaven, while excluding others, based only on their lineage? If they reject God, will they still be acceptable to Him? Does "chosen" mean "predestined" so that no matter how you live your life, God has predetermined where you will spend eternity?

Some of the answers are found in this section, and the rest throughout this book. But I will give you a big hint. The answer is no. God chose them to reveal Himself to a confused world.

Origin

While Genesis, the first book of the Bible, goes back to the creation of the world, we can trace the origins of Judaism to a man named Abraham. He lived approximately 2000 B.C. Some scholars place the origin of Judaism about 1500 B.C. to coincide with the exodus from Egypt.

At the time, there was much confusion in the world. Many people, regardless of where they lived, realized there must be a God or gods. They could see it in the creation, and the forces of nature. For example, they began to worship the Sun and the Moon. Some were worshiping the elements like the earth, fire, water, and wind. Then they expanded these to include other gods like those of the harvest, fertility, etc. It was not long before they created idols to worship.

All of this was very upsetting to the one and only God, the creator. The Bible tells us He is jealous. According to scripture, God was looking for a person of faith and he found Abraham. His faith was accounted to him for righteousness. God chose him as a conduit; that through him, the world would know God, and through his descendants, the whole world might be blessed.

The promise to Abraham was that his wife Sarah would bear a child, and that through him he would be the father of many nations. To gain a better appreciation of the promise and miracle, both Abraham and Sarah were advanced in years, and well past the time of childbearing. Nevertheless, as God had promised, Sarah bore a son, and they called him Isaac.

One of Isaac's sons was Jacob, whose name was changed to Israel. He had twelve descendants, commonly known as the "Twelve Tribes of Israel." Through one of the twelve, Joseph, they would be drawn to Egypt to fulfill God's higher purpose.

God had foreordained them to be a light unto the world. However, before they would serve Him, He would prepare them.

Gen 15:13-14

13 Then the LORD said to him, "Know for certain that your descendants will be strangers in a country not their own, and they will be enslaved and mistreated four hundred years. 14 But I will punish the nation they serve as slaves, and afterward they will come out with great possessions. "NIV"

After living four hundred years under bondage, the people should have been ready to seek God who could save them. When the time was right, He called Moses to lead them.

Moses, the prophet.

The story of Moses' life is remarkable and makes for interesting reading. He came into prominence by performing a series of miracles; thereby convincing the Egyptian Pharaoh to free the Hebrew slaves.

Moses recorded the laws and ordinances of God, for the first time, in the Torah. *Torah* is a Hebrew word meaning "teaching," "instruction," or "law." Moses is also credited with writing Exodus, Leviticus, Numbers and Deuteronomy by the inspiration of God. Together with Genesis, these make up the first five books of the Bible, also known as the Pentateuch.

Basic beliefs

They believe in one God, and that He revealed Himself to Abraham their patriarch. Though childless at the time, God chose him to be the father of many descendants, directing him to teach them to do what is just and right.

Gen 18:19

For I have chosen him, so that he will direct his children and his household after him to keep the way of the LORD by doing what is right and just, so that the LORD will bring about for Abraham what he has promised him." "NIV"

God is sovereign. He established laws and rules of conduct. When observed, people receive blessings. However, when ignored or violated, people are punished. The consequences can be immediate. However, there are many instances in the Bible where God warned the people, giving them a chance to change their ways. He was very patient, not wanting to inflict punishment.

The picture comes to mind of a father who warns their child not to touch a hot stove. After several warnings that go ignored, he spanks his child. It hurts him to do so, but he needs to get their attention, because he does not want them to suffer a greater harm.

Life is meaningless without a relationship with God. To begin with, we need to develop a healthy fear of the Almighty God. As He is sovereign, we can expect justice and hope for mercy. We please God and can expect blessings by observing His laws and ordinances and doing good deeds. On the other hand, we can expect His wrath to repay the evil we do.

They continue to look for the Messiah (Christ), the Anointed one.

Messiah is from the Hebrew and is translated as the "Anointed" one. *Christ* is from the Greek "Christos," which is the equivalent of Messiah. The mission of the Messiah is two-fold; atone for our sins and establish God's kingdom on earth.

Atonement by one definition means:

> *The act by which God restores a relationship of harmony and unity between Himself and human beings. (From Nelson's Illustrated Bible Dictionary, Copyright (c)1986, Thomas Nelson Publishers)*

Our sin, and imperfection, separates us from a Holy God who is perfect and without sin. God is just and must punish sin, yet He is also merciful and does not want to punish us. The good news is that we do not have to suffer and die for our sins because God provides a substitute for us. The *righteous* Messiah takes our place and receives the punishment that we, *the unrighteous*, deserve.

Beyond that, *atonement* means cleansing us from our sins, in the eyes of God, just as though we had never sinned. This is necessary because we cannot enter heaven and be in the presence of a Holy God unless we have been sanctified.

Sanctification by one definition means:

> *The Greek word translated "sanctification" (hagiasmos) means "holiness." To sanctify, therefore, means, "to make holy." Evangelical Dictionary of Biblical Theology. Copyright 1996 by Baker Books. All rights reserved. Used by permission.*

Typically, Jews reject Jesus because they believe that if he were the Messiah, he would have established himself as King of the Jews and ruled over the whole earth. However, let us consider that from a different perspective. To accomplish this dual mission of atonement and ruler, some Hebrew scholars have suggested there may be two Messiahs. However, scripture tells us there is one Messiah who comes twice. First, He comes to atone for our sins, and the second time as judge and ruler.

Does it matter how we live our life?

Yes! Through Moses, God gave extremely specific instructions for our conduct. He established laws and holds us accountable when we break them. God is just and has determined that we must pay a price for our sins. For example:

> *Lev 24:19-22*
>
> *19 If anyone injures his neighbor, whatever he has done must be done to him: 20 fracture for fracture, eye for eye, tooth for tooth. As he has injured the other, so he is to be injured. 21 Whoever kills an animal must make restitution, but whoever kills a man must be put to death. "NIV"*

Establishing restitution or punishment accomplished two things. First, God was discouraging those with evil intent, and secondly, He was demonstrating His love and concern for the victims.

Are you rewarded for good works?

Yes! Many believe in an active relationship with God. Quite often, as recorded in the Torah, or Old Testament of the Bible, God promises blessings for being obedient and doing what is right.

What are they striving for?

The goal of practitioners is pleasing God. Whether your rewards and punishments come here or hereafter is not relevant. Far beyond the Ten Commandments that most of us are familiar with, God has given many more laws and ordinances. He has instituted many special days, weeks, and years to be observed. If you obey all these things, it will please God. If you do not, you will pay the consequences.

What happens when we die?

Today, there is a broad difference in the beliefs and practices of those identifying themselves as Orthodox, Conservative and Reformed. While some might question life after death, they would likely agree on a relationship to and/or with God during our lifetime.

Many believe that we can earn an eternal place with God, by following the laws of Moses. On the other end of the spectrum are those that believe it is all about here and now.

However, not everyone who practices Judaism believes in life after death. In Biblical times, there were to distinct groups who held themselves up as teachers and observers of the law, the Sadducees, and the Pharisees. You can remember the difference with a little play on words. They were "Sad-you-sees" because they did not believe in the resurrection.

What is the appeal?

Typically, the people practicing Judaism are not trying to convert people to their faith. The appeal might be that there is a structure presented by which we can have a relationship with God. There is also an appeal because of a long-awaited Messiah, who is to establish God's kingdom on earth.

What are some apparent problems with this set of beliefs?

That God would choose one group at the exclusion of everyone else.

They limit their beliefs about the Messiah to one who will establish God's kingdom on earth. They further limit that to a physical kingdom. They miss the point as illustrated in the "Passover" and "Yom Kippur," that God provides a substitute to stand in our place and receive the consequence of our sins.

What does the Bible tell us?

There are times when God makes a covenant with people, either conditionally or unconditionally.

Covenant

An agreement between two people or two groups that involves promises on the part of each to the other. The concept of covenant between God and His people is one of the most important theological truths of the Bible. By making a covenant with Abraham, God promised to bless His descendants and to make them His special people. Abraham, in return, was to remain faithful to God and to serve as a channel through which God's blessings could flow to the rest of the world (Gen 12:1-3).

Even before Abraham's time, God also made a covenant with Noah, assuring Noah that He would not again destroy the world by flood (Gen 9).

(From Nelson's Illustrated Bible Dictionary, Copyright (c)1986, Thomas Nelson Publishers)

When God made a covenant with Abraham, that through his descendants the rest of the world would be blessed, it was unconditional. Just as when He promised Noah regarding another flood. These were promises made by God that would be kept no matter what.

The Bible is also full of conditional covenants. God either promises blessings for those who do what is right and pleasing to Him or promises punishment for the disobedient. Fortunately for us, God is also merciful. There is more on this in the section about God.

The Messiah has come and atoned for our sins.

Symbolism for the atonement is found in scripture. Jews, Muslims, and Christians believe that Abraham was to offer his son as a sacrifice but at the last minute, God provided a substitute animal whose blood was shed in place of Abraham's son.

Gen 22:6-14

6 Abraham took the wood for the burnt offering and placed it on his son Isaac, and he himself carried the fire and the knife. As the two of them went on together, 7 Isaac spoke up and said to his father Abraham, "Father?" "Yes, my son?" Abraham replied.

"The fire and wood are here," Isaac said, "but where is the lamb for the burnt offering?" 8 Abraham answered, "God himself will provide the lamb for the burnt offering, my son." And the two of them went on together.

9 When they reached the place God had told him about, Abraham built an altar there and arranged the wood on it. He bound his son Isaac and laid him on the altar, on top of the wood. 10 Then he reached out his hand and took the knife to slay his son. 11 But the angel of the LORD called out to him from heaven, "Abraham! Abraham!" "Here I am," he replied.

12 "Do not lay a hand on the boy," he said. "Do not do anything to him. Now I know that you fear God, because you have not withheld from me your son, your only son."

13 Abraham looked up and there in a thicket he saw a ram caught by its horns. He went over and took the ram and sacrificed it as a burnt offering instead of his son. 14 So Abraham called that place The LORD Will Provide. And to this day it is said, "On the mountain of the LORD it will be provided." "NIV"

The point is that Abraham's son was spared because God provided the substitute sacrifice.

The significance of the Passover.

There is similar symbolism as the Hebrew slaves in Egypt were saved from death by the blood of a Passover lamb.

Ex 12:21-27

21 Then Moses summoned all the elders of Israel and said to them, "Go at once and select the animals for your families and slaughter the Passover lamb. 22 Take a bunch of hyssop, dip it into the blood in the basin and put some of the blood on the top and on both sides of the doorframe. Not one of you shall go out the door of his house until morning. 23 When the LORD goes through the land to strike down the Egyptians, he will see the blood on the top and sides of the doorframe and will pass over that doorway, and he will not permit the destroyer to enter your houses and strike you down.

The Passover ceremony is a lasting reminder of how the people were saved.

24 "Obey these instructions as a lasting ordinance for you and your descendants. 25 When you enter the land that the LORD will give you as he promised, observe this ceremony. 26 And when your children ask you, 'What does this ceremony mean to you?' 27 then tell them, 'It is the Passover sacrifice to the LORD, who passed over the houses of the Israelites in

> Egypt and spared our homes when he struck down the Egyptians.'" "NIV"

The sins of those failing to celebrate the Passover were not forgiven.

> Num 9:13
>
> 13 But if a man who is ceremonially clean and not on a journey fails to celebrate the Passover, that person must be cut off from his people because he did not present the LORD's offering at the appointed time. That man will bear the consequences of his sin. "NIV"

Yom Kippur; The Day of Atonement.

The Day of Atonement demonstrates that God is just, and merciful.

The penalty for sin is death, but God loves us and does not want to punish us. Therefore, God provides a way for our sins to be removed, that we may appear before God just as though we had never sinned. Just as when the son of Abraham was to be offered as a sacrifice and God provided a substitute.

> Lev 16:6-10
>
> 6 "Aaron is to offer the bull for his own sin offering to make atonement for himself and his household. 7 Then he is to take the two goats and present them before the LORD at the entrance to the Tent of Meeting. 8 He is to cast lots for the two goats--one lot for the LORD and the other for the scapegoat. 9 Aaron shall bring the goat whose lot falls to the LORD and sacrifice it for a sin offering. 10 But the goat chosen by lot as the scapegoat shall be presented alive before the LORD to be used for making atonement by sending it into the desert as a scapegoat. "NIV"

Lev 16:15

15 "He shall then slaughter the goat for the sin offering for the people and take its blood behind the curtain and do with it as he did with the bull's blood: He shall sprinkle it on the atonement cover and in front of it. "NIV"

Lev 16:20-22

20 "When Aaron has finished making atonement for the Most Holy Place, the Tent of Meeting and the altar, he shall bring forward the live goat. 21 He is to lay both hands on the head of the live goat and confess over it all the wickedness and rebellion of the Israelites--all their sins--and put them on the goat's head. He shall send the goat away into the desert in the care of a man appointed for the task. 22 The goat will carry on itself all their sins to a solitary place; and the man shall release it in the desert. "NIV"

The Lamb of God, the scapegoat, died to atone for the sins of those who believe.

Not everyone will be saved. In Egypt, the blood of the lamb over the doorway did not save everyone, only those inside. Likewise, the sins remain for those who did not observe Passover and for those who were not in the congregation when the sins were transferred to the scapegoat on the Day of Atonement. In each case, the people were putting their faith in the Lord to save them.

Jesus was the Lamb of God, our scapegoat, as prophesied by Isaiah.

He was disfigured as he suffered and died for our sins.

Isa 52:13-14

13 See, my Servant shall prosper; he shall be highly exalted. 14 Yet many shall be amazed when they see him-yes, even far-off foreign nations and their kings; they shall stand dumbfounded, speechless in his presence. For they shall see and understand what they had not been told before. They shall see my Servant beaten and bloodied, so disfigured one would scarcely know it was a person standing there. So shall he cleanse many nations. "TLB"

His blood was sprinkled on the mercy seat that covers the arc of the covenant in heaven. The arc contains the law. The blood, sprinkled on the mercy seat, satisfied the requirements of the law, showing the consequences of sin had been paid, or atoned for.

He was not some charismatic leader. In fact, he was not esteemed at all.

Isa 53:2-3

He had no beauty or majesty to attract us to him, nothing in his appearance that we should desire him. 3 He was despised and rejected by men, a man of sorrows, and familiar with suffering. Like one from whom men hide their faces he was despised, and we esteemed him not. "NIV"

He suffered the punishment that we deserve.

Isa 53:4-5

Surely, he took up our infirmities and carried our sorrows, yet we considered him stricken by God, smitten by him, and afflicted. 5 But he was pierced for our transgressions, he was crushed for our iniquities;

the punishment that brought us peace was upon him, and by his wounds, we are healed. "NIV"

Why would the Son of God have to suffer and die for us?

As the last verse illustrates, our sins are transferred to Jesus as they were to the scapegoat.

Isa 53:6

6 We all, like sheep, have gone astray, each of us has turned to his own way;

and the LORD has laid on him the iniquity of us all. "NIV"

Because if we are punished for our sins, that is only justice.

It does not change the fact that we are guilty. We are only punished, as we deserve. We would still be unholy and destined to spend our life in hell apart from the presence of a Holy God.

However, if our sins are transferred to Him, we no longer deserve punishment.

If Jesus, who was without sin, takes upon himself our sins, they are transferred to him like with the scapegoat, and we are sinless in God's sight. We are justified before God, just as though we had never sinned, and may enter into heaven.

The good news of Jesus is:

He accepted his role as "The Lamb of God."

Because he was without sin, he was the acceptable sacrifice. He offered himself to suffer and die, as payment for the sins of others.

Isa 53:7-12

7 He was oppressed and afflicted, yet he did not open his mouth; he was led like a lamb to the slaughter, and as a sheep before her shearers is silent, so he did not open his mouth. 8 By oppression and judgment he was taken away. And who can speak of his descendants? For he was cut off from the land of the living; for the transgression of my people he was stricken. 9 He was assigned a grave with the wicked, and with the rich in his death, though he had done no violence, nor was any deceit in his mouth.

10 Yet it was the LORD's will to crush him and cause him to suffer, and though the LORD makes his life a guilt offering, he will see his offspring and prolong his days, and the will of the LORD will prosper in his hand. 11 After the suffering of his soul, he will see the light [of life] and be satisfied; by his knowledge, my righteous servant will justify many, and he will bear their iniquities. 12 Therefore I will give him a portion among the great, and he will divide the spoils with the strong, because he poured out his life unto death, and was numbered with the transgressors. For he bore the sin of many and made intercession for the transgressors. "NIV"

I really hope and pray that you get the significance of this. It is what it is all about. He who was without sin, had no reason to be punished. Therefore, he was in the unique position to receive the punishment that we deserve.

The Bible talks about the Messiah, his mission on earth, and how we can identify him. He has come once to satisfy the requirements of the law, paying the price for our sins for whoever believes. He will come again, as the Lion of Judah, judging the world and establishing his rule on earth.

You can take your chances at judgment or accept a pardon beforehand.

This should be a no-brainer. Either you risk being condemned to spend eternity suffering in hell, or you acknowledge your sin, and accept forgiveness.

John 5:24-25

> 24 "I say emphatically that anyone who listens to my message and believes in God who sent me has eternal life, and will never be damned for his sins, but has already passed out of death into life.
>
> 25 "And I solemnly declare that the time is coming, in fact, it is here, when the dead shall hear my voice- the voice of the Son of God-and those who listen shall live. "TLB"

However, anyone who is offered a pardon, and rejects it, will be worse off than never hearing it at all.

Luke 10:13-16

> 13 What horrors await you, you cities of Chorazin and Bethsaida! For if the miracles I did for you had been done in the cities of Tyre and Sidon, their people would have sat in deep repentance long ago, clothed in sackcloth and throwing ashes on their heads to show their remorse. 14 Yes, Tyre and Sidon will receive less punishment on the Judgment Day than you. 15 And you people of Capernaum, what shall I say about you? Will you be exalted to heaven? No, you shall be brought down to hell."
>
> 16 Then he said to the disciples, "Those who welcome

you are welcoming me. And those who reject you are rejecting me. And those who reject me are rejecting God who sent me." "TLB"

To my Jewish friends the choice is yours. It is an individual decision. You can accept that Jesus, *Yeshua,* is the Messiah and came to atone for your sins as the "Lamb of God." After his death and burial, he was resurrected. After many days and being seen by as many as five hundred at one time, he ascended to heaven as our high priest. He is ever ready to make intercession for us, defending us against the *Accuser,* Satan, before the Righteous Judge. Alternatively, if you reject him, you will be alone to give account of yourself before a Holy God who expects nothing less than perfection.

The Bible tells us that when he returns, it will be as the "Lion of Judah," bringing judgment and establishing his reign on earth. However, if you wait until then to accept him, it will be too late.

Roman Catholicism

Introduction

The largest of the world's religions is Christianity, of that, it is estimated that 80% are Catholic. However, that number may include both Roman Catholic, Orthodox, and splinter denominations. Within Christianity, there are groups that broke away from the Catholic Church. While a number of reasons could be sited, the main difference is that Protestants believe in "Scripture Alone," while the Catholic Church teaches "Scripture and Tradition." In this context, tradition means additional teachings not found in the Bible. Maybe the most controversial is the elevation of Mary, the mother of Jesus to such a position of prominence. As we shall see, a number of popes have embellished, even changing, what we read about her in the Bible. Her larger-than-life status appears to be the result of circular reasoning. This will be discussed later in this section.

Origin

About 2,000 years ago, Jesus started his public ministry. He attracted crowds by both the miracles he performed and the things he taught. Those who accepted his teachings became disciples.

> *Disciple (di-si'-p'-l):*
>
> *(1) Usually a substantive (mathetes, "a learner," from manthano, "to learn"; Latin discipulus, "a scholar"): The word is found in the Bible only in the Gospels and Acts. But it is good Greek, in use from Herodotus down, and always means the pupil of someone, in contrast to the master or teacher (didaskalos). See Matt 10:24; Luke 6:40. In all cases it implies that the person not only accepts the views of the teacher, but that he is also in practice an adherent.*
>
> *(From International Standard Bible Encyclopedia, Electronic Database Copyright (c)1996 by Biblesoft)*

Notice that more than believing, it is adhering, or putting what they learned into practice.

According to tradition, Peter was the first leader, or pope of the Catholic Church. Jesus selected Peter, from among his disciples, to be one of the original twelve Apostles.

> *Apostle. (Gk. apostolos). Envoy, ambassador, or messenger commissioned to carry out the instructions of the commissioning agent.*
>
> *Evangelical Dictionary of Biblical Theology. Copyright 1996 by Baker Books. All rights reserved. Used by permission.*

On what basis does the Catholic Church claim to be set apart from other religions?

The Catholic Church places great emphasis on two particular incidences recorded in the Bible. The first is commonly referred to as the confession of faith.

The Confession of Faith.

Matt 16:13-20

13 When Jesus came to the region of Caesarea Philippi, he asked his disciples, "Who do people say the Son of Man is?"

14 They replied, "Some say John the Baptist; others say Elijah; and still others, Jeremiah or one of the prophets."

15 "But what about you?" he asked. "Who do you say I am?"

16 Simon Peter answered, "You are the Christ, the Son of the living God."

17 Jesus replied, "Blessed are you, Simon son of Jonah, for this was not revealed to you by man, but by my Father in heaven. 18 And I tell you that you are Peter, and on this rock, I will build my church, and the gates of Hades will not overcome it. 19 I will give you the keys of the kingdom of heaven; whatever you bind on earth will be bound in heaven, and whatever you loose on earth will be loosed in heaven." "NIV"

A few things about this passage have caused disagreement between the Catholic Church and others identifying themselves as Christians. Catholics would point out that Jesus changed the name of Simon to Peter, which means *rock* in the original Greek as it was written. Therefore, they say it follows that Jesus was making a declaration that Simon, now Peter, was the rock on whom Jesus would build his church.

However, when you look at the original Greek words for Peter it was *Petros,* or smaller piece of rock, but when you look at the word rock in the original Greek it is translated as

Petra, or massive rock. Therefore, the conclusion others have drawn is that Peter had a piece of the rock or was a piece of it. His confession of faith was what Jesus was referring to. Peter was like a forerunner of things to come. He was one in many pieces of the huge number of believers who would follow in their confession of faith.

The second thing they would point to is the commission to Peter.

The commission to Peter.

John 21:14-15

14 This was now the third time Jesus appeared to his disciples after he was raised from the dead.

15 When they had finished eating, Jesus said to Simon Peter, "Simon son of John, do you truly love me more than these?"

"Yes, Lord," he said, "you know that I love you."

Jesus said, "Feed my lambs." "NIV"

Yes, Peter was one of the original twelve. He often demonstrated his faith. At one time, Jesus was walking on water to the boat the others were in. When he saw him, Peter himself got out of the boat and began walking on water toward Jesus. The account continues:

Matt 14:29-31

Then Peter got down out of the boat, walked on the water and came toward Jesus. 30 But when he saw the wind, he was afraid and, beginning to sink, cried out, "Lord, save me!"

> *31 Immediately Jesus reached out his hand and caught him. "You of little faith," he said, "why did you doubt?" "NIV"*

Then on the night of Jesus' arrest and trial, he prophesied to Peter that he would deny Jesus three times before the cock crowed, or before sunrise. Peter who had started with great faith and declaring his pledge to stand by Jesus even if it meant losing his life, became weak again. As Jesus' prophesied, Peter denied him.

Therefore, when Jesus asked Peter three times if he would feed his sheep, it may have been because he had disappointed him before. It could also have been to encourage Peter to become stronger in his faith. It does not necessarily mean that Jesus appointed Peter to lead his Church.

What did happen after this, as recorded in the Bible, is that Peter did become strong, boldly preaching about Jesus to anyone and everyone. However, he was not the only one. In fact, much of the New Testament involves Paul; his life changing experiences, missionary journeys, and encouragements and instructions to the body of believers.

What were the circumstances?

Everything centers around one person, Jesus. His public ministry began when he was 30 years old. He was not just a teacher or prophet as many people think. He claimed to be the Son of God. Not a watered-down version. Not "*a*" son, but "*the*" Son of God. Therefore, he was who he claimed to be, or he was a false prophet. He was put to death at about the age of 33 for his claim.

According to the Bible, Jesus performed many miracles such as healing people.

▶ Giving sight to people born blind.

▶ Healing cripples, some who had never walked before.

▶ Curing people of all forms of diseases including leprosy.

He performed miracles of nature.

▶ Feeding 5,000 on one occasion and 4,000 on another, with a few loaves of bread and a small amount of fish

▶ Calming a storm on the sea, where the wind and waves stopped

▶ Walking on water, and many more

He cast out demons, demonstrating he has power over the spirit world.

However, the most amazing miracles were bringing a number of people back to life after their death. This he did as a prelude to his own death burial and resurrection that he himself prophesied.

Basic beliefs:

At the head of the Catholic Church is a pope, often referred to as "The Holy Father." They believe he has the authority to act for God on earth. This authority is then passed on through their hierarchy to all those ordained into the priesthood. As an example, when a person confesses their sins to a local priest, they have the authority to grant "Absolution" for the forgiveness of sins.

As the spiritual leader, the pope is considered to connect with God in a way that no one else on earth can. Therefore, it follows; he is able to pray to God on our behalf, and to offer blessings and guidance from God. In a similar way, the words of the pope are as important as those found in the Bible.

This is significant as it helps us understand that within Catholicism, the elevation of Mary, the mother of Jesus, as co-mediator with the Father and that she has an equal role in our redemption.

Pope Pius IX, in 1854, proclaimed the "Immaculate Conception of Mary," that she was conceived without sin and lived a sinless life.

Pope Pius XII, in 1950, proclaimed the "Assumption," that she was taken directly into heaven.

Pope Leo XIII, in 1891, proclaimed, "As no man goes to the Father but by the Son, so no man goes to Christ but by his mother."

The Catholic Church has added things that are clearly not found in the Bible, and therefore, they must be questioned.

What do they teach is our relationship to God?

They believe in one God who reveals himself as Father, Son, and Holy Spirit. However, unlike others identifying themselves as Christians, we need intermediaries to speak to God for us in the form of saints, the priesthood, or Mary, the mother of Jesus.

What is the point of life?

First, faith in Jesus as the Christ is the beginning of salvation. Then we live life to the best of our ability. After death, there is hope in a resurrection, and eternal life in heaven with God. However, this is conditional upon observing the sacraments of the Church.

Does it matter how we live our life?

Catholics desire to obey God and believe He will punish us for our sins. If we confess them, He is willing to forgive us but sometimes it requires that we do something called penance to demonstrate our remorse. The longer between confessions the more our sins mount up and damage our relationship or separate us from God.

What are they striving for?

For some, it could be just serving or advancing in their highly structured priesthood.

A relatively few are promoted to sainthood, but not so much because of something they were trying to achieve. Rather, they became prominent in the church because of how they lived their life. Less common is sainthood for being associated with one or more miracles.

For the vast majority, it is just a relationship with God. They fear Him because they believe that He is just and must punish sin. Therefore, they want to avoid hell and try to please Him so that they can be with Him forever in heaven.

What happens when we die?

The Catholic faithful believe that through Jesus they will have entrance to heaven. However, before that, they will probably spend some time in purgatory, which is a place where people go to pay for any unforgiven sins.

What is the appeal?

It could be that people like the idea of intermediaries to approach God for them. The pope is thought to speak for God, and those under him can speak to God for us. Ordained priests can hear our confessions and grant forgiveness. Saints can hear our prayers and bring our requests before God. In these ways, the Catholic faithful can feel more connected to God.

The idea of purgatory seems fair and reasonable.

What are some apparent problems with this set of beliefs?

The Catholic Church has added things that are clearly not found in the Bible.

About Mary:

The "Immaculate Conception of Mary," that she was conceived without sin and lived a sinless life.

The "Assumption," that Mary was taken directly into heaven.

That Mary's role in redemption is co-equal with Christ.

That our access to God is through intermediaries.

That we need to confess our sins to a member of their priesthood or that we can pray to a saint to intercede for us.

Purgatory is not mentioned in the Bible, nor is the concept of paying for unforgiven sins after our death as a means to enter heaven.

Infant baptism.

The Catholic Church teaches that an ordained priest should baptize infants to fulfill the righteous requirements. This is wrong on a few counts as demonstrated a little later in this section.

What does the Bible tell us?

About Mary, the mother of Jesus.

Mary was blessed, but she is not involved in our redemption, nor is she co-equal to Christ in anything. In fact, Jesus said that his disciples were co-equal with his mother.

> *Matt 12:47-50*
>
> *47 Someone told him, "Your mother and brothers are standing outside, wanting to speak to you."*
>
> *48 He replied to him, "Who is my mother, and who are my brothers?" 49 Pointing to his disciples, he said, "Here are my mother and my brothers. 50 For whoever does the will of my Father in heaven is my brother and sister and mother." "NIV"*

Therefore, we see that over the years, the Catholic Church Fathers, through "Tradition" have added to the Bible. As they elevated Mary, they made her equal with Jesus; born without sin, an immaculate conception, lived a sinless life, co-equal in our redemption.

This is a good example of circular reasoning. Rather than seeking the truth, people start out with a forgone conclusion, and attempt to filter the facts to conform to their preconceived notions. Let us speculate on how their reasoning progressed based on the premise that Mary is the mother of Jesus, who is God in the flesh.

Since:

▶ Jesus was the Son of God.

▶ He was perfect and without sin.

▶ He provides a way for each of us to escape punishment for our sins.

▶ After his death, burial, and resurrection, he ascended to heaven.

▶ He intercedes on our behalf, defending us from the accuser, before God.

Therefore:

▶ Mary as mother of Jesus must be the wife of God.

▶ Since God is holy, His wife must be holy too.

▶ In order for Jesus to be conceived without sin, Mary must have been conceived without sin too.

▶ As the wife of God, and mother of Jesus, she must have remained sinless.

▶ To remain sinless, she must have remained a virgin.

▶ Since Jesus ascended to heaven, it makes sense that his mother, the wife of God, would too.

▶ Since Jesus is our mediator with the Father, then Mary must be our mediator too.

▶ Since she is the wife of God, we can go to her to intercede for us, thereby making her co-equal with Jesus in our salvation and redemption.

However, these assumptions are unfounded and the Biblical account is much different. The problem with all of this is that it makes Mary like God. No wonder that Muslims think the Trinity refers to The Father, the Son, and the Mother.

She was not sinless, nor did she remain a virgin.

The fact is, before the birth of Jesus, Mary was a virgin. However, after his birth she lived with her husband Joseph and had his children as the following verses from the Bible tells us. No one is without sin, Mary, or anyone else except Jesus.

Matt 13:55-56

55 "Isn't this the carpenter's son? Isn't his mother's name Mary, and aren't his brothers James, Joseph,

Simon, and Judas? 56 Aren't all his sisters with us? "NIV"

Salvation by no one else but Jesus.

Acts 4:12

12 Salvation is found in no one else, for there is no other name under heaven given to men by which we must be saved." "NIV"

This is only one example that shows the fallacy of men adding to scripture, and then trying to tell us what we should believe.

There is one mediator between God and man.

1 Tim 2:5

5 For there is one God and one mediator between God and men, the man Christ Jesus, "NIV"

We have a high priest in heaven who is able to intercede for us.

This is further explained in the book of Hebrews.

Heb 4:14-16

14 Therefore, since we have a great high priest who has gone through the heavens, Jesus the Son of God, let us hold firmly to the faith we profess. 15 For we do not have a high priest who is unable to sympathize with our weaknesses, but we have one who has been tempted in every way, just as we are-yet was without sin. 16 Let us then approach the throne of grace with confidence, so that we may receive mercy and find grace to help us in our time of need. "NIV"

Heb 7:24-28

24 but because Jesus lives forever, he has a permanent priesthood. 25 Therefore he is able to save completely those who come to God through him, because he always lives to intercede for them.

His sacrifice was done once, for all, when he offered himself.

26 Such a high priest meets our need-one who is holy, blameless, pure, set apart from sinners, exalted above the heavens. 27 Unlike the other high priests, he does not need to offer sacrifices day after day, first for his own sins, and then for the sins of the people. He sacrificed for their sins once for all when he offered himself. 28 For the law appoints as high priests men who are weak; but the oath, which came after the law, appointed the Son, who has been made perfect forever. "NIV"

His blood was sprinkled on the actual "mercy seat" in heaven.

Heb 9:6-27

6 When everything had been arranged like this, the priests entered regularly into the outer room to carry on their ministry. 7 But only the high priest entered the inner room, and that only once a year, and never without blood, which he offered for himself and for the sins the people had committed in ignorance.

An illustration for the present time

8 The Holy Spirit was showing by this that the way

> *into the Most Holy Place had not yet been disclosed as long as the first tabernacle was still standing. 9 This is an illustration for the present time, indicating that the gifts and sacrifices being offered were not able to clear the conscience of the worshiper. 10 They are only a matter of food and drink and various ceremonial washings-external regulations applying until the time of the new order.*

Christ, our high priest entered the perfect tabernacle in heaven.

> *11 When Christ came as high priest of the good things that are already here, he went through the greater and more perfect tabernacle that is not man-made, that is to say, not a part of this creation.*

He entered by his own blood that was not tainted by sin.

> *12 He did not enter by means of the blood of goats and calves; but he entered the Most Holy Place once for all by his own blood, having obtained eternal redemption. 13 The blood of goats and bulls and the ashes of a heifer sprinkled on those who are ceremonially unclean sanctify them so that they are outwardly clean. 14 How much more, then, will the blood of Christ, who through the eternal Spirit offered himself unblemished to God, cleanse our consciences from acts that lead to death, so that we may serve the living God!*

We are now under the new covenant of grace, because the requirements of the old covenant law, has been satisfied.

> *15 For this reason Christ is the mediator of a new covenant, that those who are called may receive the promised eternal inheritance-now that he has died as a ransom to set them free from the sins committed under*

> the first covenant.
>
> 16 In the case of a will, it is necessary to prove the death of the one who made it, 17 because a will is in force only when somebody has died; it never takes effect while the one who made it is living.

In fact, the law requires that nearly everything be cleansed with blood, and without the shedding of blood, there is no forgiveness.

> 18 This is why even the first covenant was not put into effect without blood. 19 When Moses had proclaimed every commandment of the law to all the people, he took the blood of calves, together with water, scarlet wool, and branches of hyssop, and sprinkled the scroll and all the people. 20 He said, "This is the blood of the covenant, which God has commanded you to keep." 21 In the same way, he sprinkled with the blood both the tabernacle and everything used in its ceremonies. 22 In fact, the law requires that nearly everything be cleansed with blood, and without the shedding of blood there is no forgiveness.

The man-made tabernacle and blood of animals was symbolic.

> 23 It was necessary, then, for the copies of the heavenly things to be purified with these sacrifices, but the heavenly things themselves with better sacrifices than these.

Christ entered heaven to do away with sin, by the sacrifice of himself,

> 24 For Christ did not enter a man-made sanctuary that was only a copy of the true one; he entered heaven

> *itself, now to appear for us in God's presence. 25 Nor did he enter heaven to offer himself again and again, the way the high priest enters the Most Holy Place every year with blood that is not his own. 26 Then Christ would have had to suffer many times since the creation of the world. But now he has appeared once for all at the end of the ages to do away with sin by the sacrifice of himself.*

This was done to satisfy the requirements of the law, for those that believe in him.

> *27 Just as man is destined to die once, and after that to face judgment, 28 so Christ was sacrificed once to take away the sins of many people; and he will appear a second time, not to bear sin, but to bring salvation to those who are waiting for him. "NIV"*

Christ died because it is impossible for any other blood but his to take away sin.

> *Heb 10:1-23*

> *10:1 The law is only a shadow of the good things that are coming-not the realities themselves. For this reason it can never, by the same sacrifices repeated endlessly year after year, make perfect those who draw near to worship. 2 If it could, would they not have stopped being offered? For the worshipers would have been cleansed once for all, and would no longer have felt guilty for their sins. 3 But those sacrifices are an annual reminder of sins, 4 because it is impossible for the blood of bulls and goats to take away sins.*

Therefore, we have been made holy through the sacrifice of the body of Jesus Christ.

> 5 Therefore, when Christ came into the world, he said:
>
> "Sacrifice and offering you did not desire, but a body you prepared for me; 6 with burnt offerings and sin offerings you were not pleased. 7 Then I said, 'Here I am-it is written about me in the scroll- I have come to do your will, O God.'"
>
> 8 First he said, "Sacrifices and offerings, burnt offerings and sin offerings you did not desire, nor were you pleased with them" (although the law required them to be made). 9 Then he said, "Here I am, I have come to do your will." He sets aside the first to establish the second. 10 And by that will, we have been made holy through the sacrifice of the body of Jesus Christ once for all.

By one sacrifice, he has made perfect forever those who are being made holy.

> 11 Day after day every priest stands and performs his religious duties; again and again he offers the same sacrifices, which can never take away sins. 12 But when this priest had offered for all time one sacrifice for sins, he sat down at the right hand of God. 13 Since that time he waits for his enemies to be made his footstool, 14 because by one sacrifice he has made perfect forever those who are being made holy.
>
> 15 The Holy Spirit also testifies to us about this. First he says:
>
> 16 "This is the covenant I will make with them after that time, says the Lord. I will put my laws in their hearts, and I will write them on their minds."

> *17 Then he adds:*
>
> *"Their sins and lawless acts I will remember no more."*
>
> *18 And where these have been forgiven, there is no longer any sacrifice for sin.*
>
> *19 Therefore, brothers, since we have confidence to enter the Most Holy Place by the blood of Jesus, 20 by a new and living way opened for us through the curtain, that is, his body, 21 and since we have a great priest over the house of God, 22 let us draw near to God with a sincere heart in full assurance of faith, having our hearts sprinkled to cleanse us from a guilty conscience and having our bodies washed with pure water. 23 Let us hold unswervingly to the hope we profess, for he who promised is faithful. "NIV"*

We have direct access to God.

We do not need to go through Mary or others designated as saints. Jesus said we can pray directly to God, our Father. We can also receive the gift of the Holy Spirit, who prays for us. There is more on this later in the section about God.

In the gospel of Mark, we read that the curtain of the temple was torn in two when Jesus died.

> *Mark 15:38-39*
>
> *38 The curtain of the temple was torn in two from top to bottom. 39 And when the centurion, who stood there in front of Jesus, heard his cry and saw how he died, he said, "Surely this man was the Son of God!" "NIV"*

The curtain was what separated man from entering into the presence of God in the Holy of Holies. No one could enter unless they were ceremonially clean; otherwise, they died on the spot. The fact that it was torn from top to bottom is significant. The curtain was extremely tall. If men were to have torn it, it would have been from bottom to top. Tearing it from top to bottom demonstrates it was torn by God to show that we now have access to Him because of Christs atoning death on the cross. Whoever accepts this is now clean.

Having forgiveness does not give us a license to sin.

A few verses after explaining that the sacrifice of Jesus for the forgiveness of sins was done once for all, the author of Hebrews warns us.

Heb 10:26-29

26 If we deliberately keep on sinning after we have received the knowledge of the truth, no sacrifice for sins is left, 27 but only a fearful expectation of judgment and of raging fire that will consume the enemies of God. 28 Anyone who rejected the law of Moses died without mercy on the testimony of two or three witnesses. 29 How much more severely do you think a man deserves to be punished who has trampled the Son of God under foot, who has treated as an unholy thing the blood of the covenant that sanctified him, and who has insulted the Spirit of grace? "NIV"

You cannot live like the devil and expect to be forgiven just by confessing your sins to someone whenever you feel like it, doing penance, and then just repeating the process. This amounts to sinning whenever it pleases you and purchasing forgiveness.

In Old Testament times, it would be like just buying an animal and taking it to the temple for your sin offering. It would have nothing to do with repentance. In more recent times, it reminds me of some gangster movies where people live a life of crime but show up at a confessional once a week to ask for forgiveness. Then they go back to their evil ways, including robbing and killing, a day later.

God wants us to change our ways.

Frankly, it is a lot easier confessing to a priest than to ask God for forgiveness. Just going through the motions, without emotion, will not do it. Sacrifices and offerings are not what God wants. He wants a remorseful heart. Repentance is not to be confused with penance. With *penance,* you only pay a price for your sin. With *repentance,* you change your mind. You recognize your sins, are terribly sorry for them and ask God's forgiveness. Furthermore, you make every attempt to change your ways and not commit the sin again.

Fortunately, we have an advocate with the Father.

We are instructed to avoid sin, yet as long as we live, it will be a struggle for us. If we should sin, we are encouraged by the fact that Jesus can relate to us, because he was tempted in all things, as we are. I like the way the *Living Bible* puts it.

> *1 John 2:1-2*
>
> *2:1 My little children, I am telling you this so that you will stay away from sin. But if you sin, there is someone to plead for you before the Father. His name is Jesus Christ, the one who is all that is good and who pleases God completely. 2 He is the one who took God's wrath against our sins upon himself and brought us into fellowship with God; and he is the forgiveness for our sins, and not only ours but all the world's. "TLB"*

To summarize, Jesus received the wrath of God that we deserved. This should not be taken lightly. He paid the price for our past sins and he is willing to stand up for us if we should sin again. However, he wants us to come directly to him and confess and repent. There is symbolism found at the last supper when Jesus washed the feet of his disciples. Peter offered to let Jesus wash more in order to cleanse him and fulfill all righteousness. However, all that was necessary was to remove the filth that had been acquired since their baptism.

About baptism.

The position of the Catholic Church is that infants inherit sin from their parents, who inherited it from Adam and Eve. They teach that ordained priests have the authority to forgive sins, and likewise can baptize infants to cleanse them from the original sin.

However, the Bible tells us we are to repent and be baptized for the forgiveness of our sins.

Acts 2:38

38 Peter replied, "Repent and be baptized, every one of you, in the name of Jesus Christ for the forgiveness of your sins. "NIV"

Note that before baptism, we are to repent. This is both unnecessary and impossible for an infant. They are innocent in God's eyes because they do not know right from wrong. In the second place, the forgiveness is for our personal sins, not Adam's or anyone else's.

Infant baptism does not meet God's standard.

Throughout the Bible, the emphasis is on the person being baptized, not the person baptizing them. We are to confess our sins, repent, and then be baptized. Nobody can do that for you. So the question you need to answer is, "Have you been baptized since repenting and placing your trust in Christ?"

What does God want?

To my Catholic friends, God loves you and wants a relationship with you. He knows you have been under the burden of guilt. He wants to set you free. He would like you to understand that his Son is our eternal high priest. He makes intercession for us as no one else can.

He also wants us to know that we are all guilty of sin. He does not want us to sin, but if we do, he wants us to come directly to Him and repent. He does not accept worthless offerings, like confessing one day, and living like the devil for six more. True repentance means acknowledging our sins and making a commitment to turn from them. He does not want lip service. He wants a contrite heart. When we come to Him on the level He expects, He offers us eternal rest.

There is more on these subjects throughout this book, and especially in the section on God.

Islam

Introduction

Islam is one of the historical religions associated with Abraham and the Bible. Adherents are called Muslims.

It began in what is now Saudi Arabia and from there it spread to Africa and Asia. While we often associate Muslims with Arabs, they are outnumbered three to one by non-Arab Muslims. It is now scattered around the world, with the largest number in Indonesia. With more than one billion followers, or $1/5^{th}$ of the population, it is the second largest religion. Only Christianity is larger.

Origin

The founder of Islam was Muhammad ibn Abdallah. He was born in 570 AD, in the city of Mecca. At the time, most of the people worshiped numerous gods, idols, and nature. He was disillusioned by the idolatrous practices around him. At the age of 40, about 622 AD, he claimed to have received his first vision when the archangel Gabriel came to him during a dream. This was the first in many visitations and became the basis for the writings of the Quran.

Abraham, the patriarch.

They trace their origin to Abraham through Ishmael, his first-born son. Whereas in Judaism, they trace the promise of God's blessing through Isaac, the son of Abraham and Sarah. An interesting side note is that Ishmael had twelve descendants, which is parallel to Jacob, the descendent of Isaac.

Basic beliefs.

Central to their religion is the belief in one God, Allah. They also believe in angels, the chief of which is Gabriel. There is also a fallen angel named Shaitan (Satan), who has followers, the jinns, or demons. They believe in four books:

▶ The Torah of Moses, the first five books of the Bible.

▶ The Zabur, or the Psalms of David

▶ The Injil, or Gospel of Jesus and

▶ The Quran

Of these, they believe the Quran to be the most reliable. Muslims believe that God had previously revealed Himself to the earlier prophets of the Jews and Christians, such as Abraham, Moses, David, and Jesus. Muslims accept the teachings of both the Jewish Torah and the Christian Gospels with an important exception; they do not accept Jesus as the Son of God. Since there are contradictions between the Bible and their sacred books, they believe human writers like Luke, John and Paul must have changed or corrupted the scriptures.

They believe that Islam is the perfection of the religion revealed to the prophets, the last and greatest of which was Muhammad. The Quran was reputedly revealed to Muhammad beginning about 610 AD in a series of visions over 22 years by the angel Gabriel. The Quran is divided into 114 Suras (chapters). They have since added the Hadith (traditions) that is a collection of Muhammad's teachings, doings, and practices. It is believed to be second in importance only to the Quran.

Does it matter how we live our life?

The adherents of Islam believe that God is all-powerful and seek to please Him. The word Islam means submission to the will of God. A Muslim is one that practices Islam following Muhammad and observing all things. Chief among those are the "Five Pillars of Faith,"

▶ Make a statement of belief by publicly repeating the Shahadah. "There is no God but Allah and Muhammad is the prophet of Allah."

▶ Prayer in a prescribed way, five times a day, showing obedience to Allah.

▶ Giving alms equal to 2.5% of your earnings. The money is for the benefit of the Muslim community, including support of the local mosque and providing for the poor and unfortunate.

▶ Observing Ramadan, the highest of Muslim holy seasons. Muslims are required to fast during the daylight hours abstaining from food, drink, and pleasures.

▶ Making a pilgrimage to Mecca.

What happens when we die?

They believe in a final judgment day where God will send people to heaven or hell. The Quran teaches that two angels write down all human activities. The picture comes to mind of the scales of justice. If your good deeds outweigh your bad ones, you will be sent to heaven and eternal bliss. Otherwise, you will be sent to hell and unimaginable suffering.

Your good deeds are not just random acts of kindness. The only ones that qualify are those compatible with the teaching of Islam.

What is the appeal?

Of course, many are born in a region where the dominant religion is Islam, but there are many converts too. The true adherents of Islam are living their lives in a way they believe will be pleasing to God. They are well intentioned, and maybe that is part of the appeal. Many people would like a clear idea about God and what he expects from us. Even though the laws are strict, it is nice to have a set of instructions, like a road map to heaven.

While there are differences, there are also similarities between what Muslims, Jews and Christians believe.

Feasts and observances with special meaning.

"Eid ul-Adha" (Feast of Sacrifice).

This feast commemorates the occasion recorded in Sura 37:102-107, when Allah commanded Abraham to sacrifice his son. Allah was pleased with the willingness of Abraham and provided a ram in his son's place at the last moment. At this special time, Muslims all over the world sacrifice sheep, goats, cows, and camels, to seek the favor of Allah.

Christians also believe in this event as recorded in the Bible. However, there is a special significance for Christians in that Abraham's son was spared because God provided the substitute sacrifice. A sacrifice was necessary because according to scripture:

Rom 3:23

23 for all have sinned and fall short of the glory of God, "NIV"

> *Heb 9:22*
>
> *22 In fact, the law requires that nearly everything be cleansed with blood, and without the shedding of blood there is no forgiveness. "NIV"*

There are similar symbolisms in "Passover" and "The Day of Atonement" as we saw in the section on Judaism. These special feasts and observances show that God is merciful and willing to forgive us for our sins.

> *Deut 4:31*
>
> *31 For the LORD your God is a merciful God; "NIV"*

> *Supported in Sura 2:218*

We are saved by faith as demonstrated to God by observing these special events; otherwise, there is no forgiveness. The sins of those not observing Eid ul-Adha, Passover, or The Day of Atonement, were not forgiven.

Since these special observances were done once a year, to atone for past sins, what happens if we sin again?

This is a critical question. God is just and must punish sin. Yet, He does not want to punish us. So how can He be both merciful and just?

How can we ever be sure we are acceptable to God and be allowed into His heaven and have eternal life?

God wants us to have that assurance.

1 John 5:13

13 I write these things to you who believe in the name of the Son of God so that you may know that you have eternal life. "NIV"

In the section on Catholicism, we saw that Jesus made a sacrifice that only needed to be done once. It was sufficient for everyone. However, only those who accept it may benefit from it.

Jesus is special; there is no one like him.

Muhammad was not sinless or faultless but his sins were forgiven.

"Go to Muhammad as Allah has forgiven his past and future sins." Hadith 8:570

Jesus is faultless, without sin.

Here an angel is speaking,

"He said, I am only a messenger of thy Lord, that I may bestow on thee [Mary] a faultless son [Jesus]" Sura 19:19

Jesus was born of the Virgin Mary by a special miracle.

"O Mary! Lo! Allah hath chosen thee...She said, 'My Lord! How can I have a child when no mortal has touched me?" Sura 3:42,47

Jesus performed miracles and forgave sins.

The Quran states Jesus healed the blind and lepers and raised the dead. Sura 5:110

Matt 9:2-7

2 Some men brought to him a paralytic, lying on a mat. When Jesus saw their faith, he said to the paralytic, "Take heart, son; your sins are forgiven."

3 At this, some of the teachers of the law said to themselves, "This fellow is blaspheming!"

4 Knowing their thoughts, Jesus said, "Why do you entertain evil thoughts in your hearts? 5 Which is easier: to say, 'Your sins are forgiven,' or to say, 'Get up and walk'? 6 But so that you may know that the Son of Man has authority on earth to forgive sins." . . ."Then he said to the paralytic, "Get up, take your mat and go home." 7 And the man got up and went home. "NIV"

Jesus has the power to raise the dead.

"When Allah saith: O Jesus.... heal him who was born blind and the leper...raise the dead, by my permission." Sura 5:110

Luke 7:11-17

11 Soon afterward, Jesus went to a town called Nain, and his disciples and a large crowd went along with him. 12 As he approached the town gate, a dead person was being carried out-the only son of his mother, and she was a widow. And a large crowd from the town was with her. 13 When the Lord saw her, his heart went out to her and he said, "Don't cry."

14 Then he went up and touched the coffin, and those carrying it stood still. He said, "Young man, I say to you, get up!" 15 The dead man sat up and began to talk, and Jesus gave him back to his mother.

> *16 They were all filled with awe and praised God. "A great prophet has appeared among us," they said. "God has come to help his people." 17 This news about Jesus spread throughout Judea and the surrounding country. "NIV"*

This was only one of many instances recorded in scripture where Jesus brought the dead back to life.

Jesus' own death, burial, and resurrection.

When Jesus brought others back to life, he demonstrated that he had power over life and death. He even prophesied about his own death burial and resurrection.

> *"Peace be on me the day I was born, and the day I die, and the day I shall be raised alive! Such was Jesus." Sura 19:33-34*

This is a key point.

Muslims believe this will be some future event because they have been taught that Jesus did not die on the cross. Instead, someone died in his place and Jesus ascended to heaven while still living. Therefore, they believe this must be a future event.

That is ironic. They believe someone died for Jesus while the Bible says Jesus died for us. However, notice the past, present, and future tense in the Sura. The question is, "Why not believe this has already happened as recorded in the Gospel?"

The good news of Jesus.

Jesus died for our sins, rose from the dead, is with God in heaven, and will come again. Note the emphasis that this was according to scripture, meaning prophecy fulfilled, so that we can genuinely believe it!

1 Cor 15:3-6

3 For what I received I passed on to you as of first importance: that Christ died for our sins according to the Scriptures, 4 that he was buried, that he was raised on the third day according to the Scriptures, 5 and that he appeared to Peter, and then to the Twelve. 6 After that, he appeared to more than five hundred of the brothers at the same time, most of whom are still living, "NIV"

Note that at the time this was written, the author was pointing out that many were alive who could verify they saw Jesus after his resurrection.

Mark 16:19

19 After the Lord Jesus had spoken to them, he was taken up into heaven and he sat at the right hand of God. "NIV"

Acts 1:11

11 "Men of Galilee," they said, "why do you stand here looking into the sky? This same Jesus, who has been taken from you into heaven, will come back in the same way you have seen him go into heaven." "NIV"

Jesus will descend (return) as a ruler and a judge.

Allah's Apostle said, '...son of Mary [Jesus] will shortly descend amongst you people [Muslims] as a ruler...." Hadith 3:425

"Allah's Apostle said, 'How will you be with the son of Mary [Jesus] will descend amongst you and he will judge the people...." Hadith 4:658

Matt 25:31-32

31 "When the Son of Man comes in his glory, and all the angels with him, he will sit on his throne in heavenly glory. 32 All the nations will be gathered before him, and he will separate the people one from another as a shepherd separates the sheep from the goats. "NIV"

Matt 25:34

34 "Then the King will say to those on his right, 'Come, you who are blessed by my Father; take your inheritance, the kingdom prepared for you since the creation of the world. "NIV"

Matt 25:41

41 "Then he will say to those on his left, 'Depart from me, you who are cursed, into the eternal fire prepared for the devil and his angels. "NIV"

Jesus is the Messiah or translated as the "Anointed."

In the Quran Jesus is frequently called the Messiah. For example:

"The Messiah, Jesus, Son of Mary...." Sura 4:171

It should be pointed out that *Christ* is from the Greek "Christos," which is the equivalent of Messiah.

What was Jesus anointed for?

More than a prophet, teacher, healer, miracle worker, Jesus was the only person who ever lived a sinless life. Therefore, he was in a unique position to offer himself as "The Lamb of God," our Passover Lamb. Just as in times past, the sins of the congregation observing the Day of Atonement were transferred to the scapegoat, Jesus offered himself as our scapegoat to have our sins transferred to him. Where we deserved to die, paying the price for our own sins, Jesus suffered and died in our place. He who was sinless was in the unique position to receive the punishment that we deserved.

The acceptable sacrifice to atone, or pay the price, for our sins.

Since we all have sinned, and fall short of God's standards, we all deserve punishment. Therefore, it would be justice if we were put to death and spent eternity suffering in hell.

> Rom 5:19
>
> *19 For just as through the disobedience of the one man the many were made sinners, so also through the obedience of the one man the many will be made righteous. "NIV"*

The yearly ritual of Eid ul-Adha, Passover and the Day of Atonement are necessary to show us how our sins are atoned for. The animals sacrificed were to be without spot or blemish, symbolizing without sin. They were killed, by the shedding of their blood, to atone for our sins. The reason these are yearly observances is to remind us how we can have our sins forgiven. However, these animals were not, nor can they ever be a sinless substitute for us, therefore it is an imperfect sacrifice.

A perfect sacrifice would require that someone without sin would suffer and die in our place. Jesus is the only one who is sinless and therefore, the only acceptable sacrifice. Because God is both just and merciful

> *He forgiveth whom He will and punishes whom He will. Allah is forgiving, merciful. Sura 3:129*

However, not everyone will be saved.

In Egypt, the blood of the lamb over the doorway did not save everyone, only those inside. Likewise, the sins remain for those who did not observe Passover and for those who were not in the congregation when the sins were transferred to the scapegoat on the Day of Atonement. In each case, the people were putting their faith in the Lord to save them.

> *Unless you believe that Jesus is the anointed one, and that he has paid the penalty for your sins, there is no forgiveness.*

> *John 3:36*

> *36 Whoever believes in the Son has eternal life, but whoever rejects the Son will not see life, for God's wrath remains on him." "NIV"*

What are some apparent problems with this set of beliefs?

You are never sure that you will go to heaven.

They teach that if your good deeds outweigh your bad deeds, that God will probably accept you. In that case, nobody ever really knows if they will go to heaven. That is, unless one is a martyr, or dies fighting in a jihad, or holy war.

Like others, they have accepted new revelations superseding the Bible.

Fundamentally, they accept much of the Bible, but believe the Quran is the last revelation from God. Therefore, if the Bible conflicts with their teachings, they refer to the Quran as the final word.

For example, the Bible says that Abraham was about to offer his son Isaac, but they replace Isaac with Ishmael, who was born of an Egyptian mother. As we saw with Judaism, the "who" was not important anyway. It was that God did not really want Abraham's son to be sacrificed, it was a test, and God provided a substitute.

As we shall see with Jehovah's Witnesses, Mormons and Christian Scientists, others have claimed new prophetic revelations from God. In each case, where the Bible contradicts their new teachings, they claim the Bible is in error. Either being translated incorrectly or corrupted by some of the authors. However, we still have many manuscripts written in the original Hebrew and Greek that the translators of today can refer to in verifying its reliability. This is unlike the Quran, which had many of its original manuscripts burned by the third Caliph in order to establish one version. Nevertheless, not all were burned and new early manuscript finds indicate key differences between the earliest copies of the Quran and the ones in use today.

In the Quran and the Bible, Jesus is clearly established as unique. Nobody else was faultless or performed miracles like he did. To Muslims, he was a prophet, yet Jesus himself claimed to be the Son of God and that the Spirit of God the Father was in him. Therefore, it would seem that Jesus is either who he claimed to be, or a false prophet. There is more on this throughout this book, as you will see.

What does the Bible tell us?

An everlasting, unconditional, covenant.

The Bible tells us that the promise of an everlasting covenant was established for the descendants of Isaac. He was the son born to fulfill the promise of God to Abraham.

Gen 17:18-21

18 And Abraham said to God, "If only Ishmael might live under your blessing!"

19 Then God said, "Yes, but your wife Sarah will bear you a son, and you will call him Isaac. I will establish my covenant with him as an everlasting covenant for his descendants after him. 20 And as for Ishmael, I have heard you: I will surely bless him; I will make him fruitful and will greatly increase his numbers. He will be the father of twelve rulers, and I will make him into a great nation. 21 But my covenant I will establish with Isaac, whom Sarah will bear to you by this time next year." "NIV"

It is important to note that all of us have the same God. His promise to Abraham was that he would be the father of many nations. This was an unconditional covenant, or promise, by God. His descendants were "chosen" to reveal to the rest of the world who God is. Those of us who are not direct descendants can be "grafted" in. This analogy found in the Bible is like when a branch from one plant is grafted into another. The branch becomes one with the native plant, drawing its nourishment from the roots.

In the following passage, the illustration is that those descendants of Abraham and Isaac either never believed as they should have, or they lost their faith. Either way, they were like branches that were broken off, leaving room for others to be grafted in.

Rom 11:17

17 If some of the branches have been broken off, and you, though a wild olive shoot, have been grafted in among the others and now share in the nourishing sap from the olive root, "NIV"

Therefore, we are all equal in the sight of God. He provides a way for all of us to have a relationship with Him. There are more illustrations about "the true vine" discussed later in this book and illustrated in the Bible.

We can all approach God in the same way.

We can learn much from Psalm 51 when David sought forgiveness by God. He felt genuine remorse after the prophet Nathan confronted him about his sin. Nathan used an illustration to help David see how wrong it was for him to sin with Bathsheba and cover one sin with another.

As king, David was in a position to judge. Nathan told him a story of a wealthy landowner who also owned many sheep. Nevertheless, this person was not satisfied with what they had. One of the landowner's poor but loyal servants owned one lamb. Not being content with what he had; the landowner took the lamb from his servant. Nathan then asked David what should be done with the rich man. David burned with anger and declared that the person who did this must die! Then Nathan told David that he was that man! David, who had many wives and concubines, committed adultery with Bathsheba, the wife of his loyal servant Uriah. Afterwards, to cover that sin, he arranged for Uriahs' death. David felt tremendous guilt for his sins and in his anguish, he turned to God. The following is an example to all of us.

Psalm 51, A prayer for forgiveness.

David is asking God to have mercy on him as the result of acknowledging his sins and that he deserves punishment. Put yourself in his place as you read the following passage:

Psalm 51:1-17

1 You are kind, God! Please have pity on me. You are

always merciful! Please wipe away my sins. 2 Wash me clean from all of my sin and guilt.

3 I know about my sins, and I cannot forget my terrible guilt. 4 You are really the one I have sinned against; I have disobeyed you and have done wrong. So, it is right for you to correct and punish me. 5 I have sinned and done wrong since the day I was born.

We deceive ourselves when ignoring our sins.

6 But you want complete honesty, so teach me true wisdom.

God alone cleanses us from our sins.

7 Wash me with hyssop until I am clean and whiter than snow.

What a joy to know we have forgiveness!

8 Let me be happy and joyful! You crushed my bones now let them celebrate.

9 Turn your eyes from my sin and cover my guilt.

God helps us by the power of the Holy Spirit.

10 Create pure thoughts in me and make me faithful again. 11 Don't chase me away from you or take your Holy Spirit away from me. 12 Make me as happy as you did when you saved me; make me want to obey! 13 I will teach sinners your Law, and they will return to you.

God saves.

14 Keep me from any deadly sin. Only you can save me!

God saves by grace. *

Then I will shout and sing about your power to save.

Change me by the power of your Holy Spirit.

15 Help me to speak and I will praise you, Lord.

Confessed sin and repentance.

16 Offerings and sacrifices are not what you want. 17 The way to please you is to feel sorrow deep in our hearts. This is the kind of sacrifice you won't refuse. "CEV"

What we learn from this is that:

▶ Our sins are against God.

▶ Sins cause separation from God.

▶ True repentance means acknowledging our sins and resolving to turn away from them.

▶ Asking God's help to overcome temptation and sin in the future.

▶ God saves us by grace, or unmerited favor, not by our works.

Grace

Favor or kindness shown without regard to the worth or merit of the one who receives it and in spite of what that same person deserves. Grace is one of the key attributes of God. The Lord God is "merciful and gracious, long-suffering, and abounding in goodness and truth" (Ex 34:6). Therefore, grace is almost always associated with mercy, love, compassion, and patience as the source of help and with deliverance from distress.

(From Nelson's Illustrated Bible Dictionary, Copyright (c) 1986, Thomas Nelson Publishers)

To my Muslim friends, I am convinced that, as a group, you are committed to submitting to God and doing what is right. However, there is a major difference between what Islam teaches and what the Bible tells us. You have been taught that if your good deeds outweigh your bad ones, that God is likely to accept you. While the Bible tells us our good deeds are offensive.

Isa 64:6

6 All of us have become like one who is unclean,

and all our righteous acts are like filthy rags; "NIV"

However, God provides a way through which we might be found clean. There is more on this throughout this book, and it is summarized in the section about God.

Jehovah's Witnesses

Introduction

There are currently over 6,000,000 Witnesses in 230 countries of the world. Typically, each Witness spends 10 hours each month engaged in door-to-door evangelism.

The Watchtower, their primary magazine, is used for witnessing and doctrinal instruction. It is printed in 132 languages, with a print run of 22,000,000 copies per issue. They have been effective, as converts are gained at the rate of 5500 per week.

Jehovah's Witnesses work hard to please God.

They get their name by attempting to please Jehovah, one of the Hebrew names for God, by serving as His witnesses. As a form of worship, they devote much of their time in training for and performing door-to-door evangelism or *witnessing.*

Origin

Jehovah's Witnesses are members of an international religious organization who believe they are the restoration of first-century Christianity. Founded in the 1870s by Charles Taze Russell under the name Bible Students, they underwent numerous disagreements and later adopted the name Jehovah's Witnesses in 1931 under Joseph Franklin Rutherford.

Basic beliefs.

They identify themselves as Christians, believing that Jesus is the Christ, or anointed one. However, many of their beliefs are quite different from other Christians and are contradicted by the Bible. We will consider a few.

They believe it is essential to recognize that Jehovah is the personal name of the one and only God. They reject the concept of the Trinity and teach that:

> *The Holy Spirit is not God but is God's impersonal "active force" for accomplishing His will in the world.*
>
> *"Jesus is a mighty God, but He is not God Almighty like the Father is."*

In fact, they believe Jesus was created. His pre-human existence was as Michael the Archangel. What seems confusing to me is calling Jesus a mighty God but denying the Trinity. That seems like a contradiction, unless they believe in many gods, which would put them into the category of polytheists.

They believe in prophecy and that God is using the *Watchtower Society* for revelations today. Quoting from their book *Reasoning From The Scriptures:*

> *The Watchtower Society is God's visible representative on earth and should be obeyed as the voice of God.*

They believe God uniquely inspires them and that theirs is the only true church. Therefore, you must be a Jehovah's Witness or you have no hope for salvation. Their literature states:

> *"A third requirement is that we be associated with God's channel, his organization. . . Jehovah is using only one organization today to accomplish his will. To*

receive everlasting life in the earthly Paradise we must identify that organization and serve God as part of it." (Watchtower 15 Feb 1983 p. 12)

Does it matter how we live our life?

Like other religious groups, they have incorporated a strong moral code. However, avoiding certain things is not enough. They teach that faith is necessary for salvation but works must be added to it. They place a great emphasis on "witnessing." The amount of time they spend "preaching," going door-to-door or standing in front of restaurants and other public places sharing literature, is enormous.

What are they striving for?

Jehovah's Witnesses believe that the hope for mankind is to live forever on a paradise earth. The hope for the dead is the resurrection to life on the restored earth.

What happens when we die?

The Witnesses deny the existence of hell. That means there is no eternal punishment. All non-Witnesses are just annihilated immediately upon death.

Jehovah's Witnesses put forth the idea that baptized believers are classified into two groups. The first is called the *anointed* class or *the little flock.* These are limited in number to 144,000 and are considered *God's sons* and *joint heirs* with the Son of God, Christ Jesus. Consequently, they will co-rule with him in the "kingdom of heavens." This class, therefore, has the hope of entering heaven after death.

The other class according to Jehovah's Witnesses' beliefs was identified in 1935 and was then called the *Jonadab class.* Today they are referred to as the *other sheep,* based on a passage in John 10:16 where Jesus speaks of having "other sheep... that are not of this fold." This identification for the "other sheep" differs radically from the current mainstream view of this passage, namely that Jesus would bring his Jewish believers (little flock) and Gentile believers (other sheep) together into one-fold.

This "other sheep" class of Jehovah's Witnesses makes up more than 99% of their believers today. Though they are not *born again* as reigning *kings and priests* in God's heavenly kingdom, they anticipate being subjects of God's kingdom, enjoying everlasting life on a peaceful, paradisiacal earth. This doctrine of two classes of believers is unique to Jehovah's Witnesses.

What is the appeal?

There is comfort in feeling connected with God through modern day revelations and prophecy. They appear incredibly happy to be involved in their life's work, to share their faith with others.

What are some apparent problems with this set of beliefs?

They have a history of false prophecies.

For example:

▶ They predicted that in 1874 the second coming of Christ would occur.

▶ They predicted that 1914 would mark the overthrow of human governments and that God would establish His kingdom on earth.

▶ They predicted that in 1925 some Old Testament saints would be resurrected and live in California.

▶ They also predicted that in 1975 the thousand-year reign of Christ would begin.

How do they defend their false prophecies?

When prophecy is not fulfilled, or when their earlier leaders like Joseph Rutherford, whose writings and doctrines are found to be contradictory, they are dismissed by the Watchtower Society as inconsistent with the current progressive light.

In other words, they would like us to believe that just because a whole succession of prophesies were false, that does not mean they are false prophets. Rather they would like us to excuse that by believing that God is revealing more all the time. It should not matter if they got it wrong because they will get it right eventually.

Additionally, when what the Witnesses teach is inconsistent with the Bible, just like Muslims and Mormons, they say that the Bible is not reliable. However, as we saw earlier, just the opposite is true. Unlike the Quran, Book of Mormon, and literature produced by the Watchtower Society, the Bible is reliable and stands up under scrutiny.

False prophecies are really indefensible.

The Bible tells us how to determine whether a prophet is true or not.

Deut 18:22

22 when a prophet speaketh in the name of Jehovah, if the thing follow not, nor come to pass, that is the thing which Jehovah hath not spoken: the prophet hath spoken it presumptuously, thou shalt not be afraid of him. "ASV"

If their prophecies are false, we need to question everything they teach.

What does the Bible tell us?

About God?

As we saw in the beginning of this section, the Bible does tell us, there is only one God.

> *Deut 6:4*
>
> *4 Hear, O Israel: The LORD our God, the LORD is one. "NIV"*

Looking at the original Hebrew in this passage, the word for LORD is Yahweh, and the word for God is Elohiym. However, God has declared giving Him a name is not what is important. Rather, it is recognizing that there is only one God. There is more on this in the section about Mormons, Christian Scientists and about God.

About the trinity?

The Witnesses teach:

> *"There can't be three Gods in one God, or three Gods in one person."*

However that is a misunderstanding because mainstream Christianity teaches there is one God who displays Himself in three persons as illustrated in the following passage and in many more throughout this book.

> *Matt 3:16-17*
>
> *16 As soon as Jesus was baptized, he went up out of the water. At that moment, heaven was opened, and he saw the Spirit of God descending like a dove and lighting on him. 17 And a voice from heaven said, "This is my Son, whom I love; with him I am well pleased." "NIV"*

All three have a part in our salvation.

Matt 28:19

19 Therefore go and make disciples of all nations, baptizing them in the name of the Father and of the Son and of the Holy Spirit, "NIV"

There is more on this in the section about God.

About Jesus?

They believe he was God's first creation. His pre-human, or pre-incarnate, existence was as Michael the Archangel. On the contrary, the Bible tells us that Jesus is the exact likeness of God, and He was the creator; he was not created.

Col 1:15-17

15 Christ is the exact likeness of the unseen God. He existed before God made anything at all, and, in fact, 16 Christ himself is the Creator who made everything in heaven and earth, the things we can see and the things we can't; the spirit world with its kings and kingdoms, its rulers and authorities; all were made by Christ for his own use and glory. 17 He was before all else began and it is his power that holds everything together. "TLB"

The Bible is clear that Jesus is not an angel.

Heb 1:5-6

5 For to which of the angels did God ever say, "You are my Son; today I have become your Father"? Or again, "I will be his Father, and he will be my Son"? 6 And again, when God brings his firstborn into the world, he says, "Let all God's angels worship him." "NIV"

Jesus, the Son, is God.

Continuing in the same passage

Heb 1:8-9

8 But about the Son he says, "Your throne, O God, will last for ever and ever, and righteousness will be the scepter of your kingdom. 9 You have loved righteousness and hated wickedness; therefore God, your God, has set you above your companions by anointing you with the oil of joy." "NIV"

John 1:1

1:1 In the beginning was the Word, and the Word was with God, and the Word was God. "NIV"

John 1:14-18

14 The Word became flesh and made his dwelling among us. We have seen his glory, the glory of the One and Only, who came from the Father, full of grace and truth.

15 John testifies concerning him. He cries out, saying, "This was he of whom I said, 'He who comes after me has surpassed me because he was before me.' "16 From the fullness of his grace we have all received one blessing after another. 17 For the law was given through Moses; grace and truth came through Jesus Christ. 18 No one has ever seen God, but God the One and Only, who is at the Father's side, has made him known. "NIV"

He is in very nature God, who became like us.

Jesus is not a separate God or lesser God; he has the very nature of God.

Phil 2:6-8

6 Who, being in very nature God, did not consider equality with God something to be grasped, 7 but made himself nothing, taking the very nature of a servant, being made in human likeness. 8 And being found in appearance as a man, he humbled himself and became obedient to death-even death on a cross! "NIV"

When he became like us, in human form, he did not become a lesser God.

Rather he gave up some of the attributes of God. In his human form, he was no longer:

▶ "Omnipresent," or everywhere at once, in human form, he was limited to space and time.

▶ He was no longer "Omniscient," knowing everything. He was often in prayer, communing with God the Father

▶ He was not "Omnipotent;" or all-powerful. He did perform miracles, and at any time, he could have called legions of angels, but he submitted himself to the will of the Father.

He gave up some of the attributes of God to be tempted as we are.

This fact is what makes Jesus worthy as "The Lamb of God" to bear the consequence of our sin. If it were not possible for Him to sin, it would not make any difference if he were tempted or not. However, being tempted, He can relate to us because He knows what it is like. Yet, being tempted, he remained sinless. Therefore, we are all without an excuse since we all have given in to temptation.

Jesus is Lord, to the glory of God the Father.

Continuing in the same passage:

Phil 2:9-11

9 Therefore God exalted him to the highest place and gave him the name that is above every name, 10 that at the name of Jesus every knee should bow, in heaven and on earth and under the earth, 11 and every tongue confess that Jesus Christ is Lord, to the glory of God the Father. "NIV"

Jesus said that the spirit of Jehovah, God the Father, is in him

When asked by Philip, one of his disciples, Jesus states further evidence regarding the Trinity.

John 14:8-11

8 Philip said, "Lord, show us the Father and that will be enough for us."

9 Jesus answered: "Don't you know me, Philip, even after I have been among you such a long time? Anyone who has seen me has seen the Father. How can you say, 'Show us the Father'? 10 Don't you believe that I am in the Father, and that the Father is in me? The words I say to you are not just my own. Rather, it is the Father, living in me, who is doing his work. 11 Believe me when I say that I am in the Father and the Father is in me; or at least believe on the evidence of the miracles themselves. "NIV"

There is more on this later in the sections for Christian Scientists and about God.

Other problems for Jehovah's Witnesses.

They do not believe in the physical resurrection.

Jehovah's Witnesses also teach that after his death God raised him as an immortal spirit without a physical body. However, the Bible says Jesus was resurrected with a body, not just as a spirit.

John 20:27-28

27 Then he said to Thomas, "Put your finger here; see my hands. Reach out your hand and put it into my side. Stop doubting and believe." 28 Thomas said to him, "My Lord and my God!" "NIV"

There is more evidence for this in the section on Hinduism and about God.

About hell.

The Witnesses deny the existence of hell. That means there is no eternal punishment. All non-Witnesses are just annihilated immediately upon death. However, the Bible warns us that hell is real, and we should fear it!

▶ All unsaved go there.

▶ People are conscious.

▶ Their senses suffer.

▶ They are in agony.

▶ They have a memory with mental and emotional regrets.

▶ There is not a second chance or communication with the living to warn and motivate others to repent.

▶ It is a place of punishment.

▶ It is a terrible place for all eternity.

You can see by the following passages that hell is real, and you do not want you or your friends and loved ones to go there.

Mark 9:47-48

47 And if your eye causes you to sin, pluck it out. It is better for you to enter the kingdom of God with one eye than to have two eyes and be thrown into hell, 48 where "'their worm does not die, and the fire is not quenched.' "NIV"

Luke 12:5

5 But I will show you whom you should fear: Fear him who, after the killing of the body, has power to throw you into hell. Yes, I tell you, fear him. "NIV"

Luke 16:22-31

22 "The time came when the beggar died and the angels carried him to Abraham's side. The rich man also died and was buried. 23 In hell, where he was in torment, he looked up and saw Abraham far away, with Lazarus by his side. 24 So he called to him, 'Father Abraham, have pity on me and send Lazarus to dip the tip of his finger in water and cool my tongue, because I am in agony in this fire.'

25 "But Abraham replied, 'Son, remember that in your lifetime you received your good things, while Lazarus received bad things, but now he is comforted here and you are in agony. 26 And besides all this, between us and you a great chasm has been fixed, so that those who want to go from here to you cannot, nor can anyone cross over from there to us.'

27 "He answered, 'Then I beg you, father, send Lazarus to my father's house, 28 for I have five brothers. Let him warn them, so that they will not also come to this place of torment.'

> 29 "Abraham replied, 'They have Moses and the Prophets; let them listen to them.' 30 "'No, father Abraham,' he said, 'but if someone from the dead goes to them, they will repent.' 31 "He said to him, 'If they do not listen to Moses and the Prophets, they will not be convinced even if someone rises from the dead.'" "NIV"

About salvation or being saved.

The Witnesses believe that Christ's death did not pay the penalty for our personal sin, but it brought about the possibility for our perfection in this life. They believe that sin is falling short of God's perfection. All humans inherit sin from Adam and Eve. When Jesus was crucified, it atoned, or paid the price, for our inherited sin but not our individual sin. The Witnesses teach that you earn salvation by your hard work and performing good deeds and total obedience to the Watchtower Society. This is quite different from what we read in the Bible.

The Bible tells us that Christ died so that whoever believes should not perish. There is not a general salvation for everyone; it is conditional, based on our faith.

> John 3:16

> 16 "For God so loved the world that he gave his one and only Son, that whoever believes in him shall not perish but have eternal life "NIV"

> John 3:18

> 18 Whoever believes in him is not condemned, but whoever does not believe stands condemned already because he has not believed in the name of God's one and only Son. "NIV"

John 3:36

36 Whoever believes in the Son has eternal life, but whoever rejects the Son will not see life, for God's wrath remains on them. "NIV"

The Bible says we are saved by our faith alone.

Acts 16:30-31

30 He then brought them out and asked, "Sirs, what must I do to be saved?" 31 They replied, "Believe in the Lord Jesus, and you will be saved-you and your household." "NIV"

To my friends who identify themselves as Jehovah's Witnesses, do not be deceived. The Watchtower Society is not the only group who has claimed further revelation from God that takes precedence over the Bible. However, the Bible can be substantiated while unfulfilled prophecy should bring into question your leadership.

Hell is real and you do not want to go there. Our salvation is a result of grace, or unmerited favor, for all who place their trust in Jesus. True, we are encouraged to live our life in a way that pleases God by serving others, but that is not what saves us. There is more on this throughout this book, and especially in the sections about Mormonism and about God.

Section II

Polytheists: those that believe in many gods.

We usually associate ancient civilizations like the Egyptians, Greeks, and Romans with their many gods. However, even today we have some well-known religions that are polytheistic. We will look at Hinduism because of the large number of followers, and its influence on other religious groups.

We will also look at Mormonism. Although relatively small in numbers, the Mormons have achieved a certain amount of notoriety. Yet, most people are not aware that they believe in many Gods or their doctrine of eternal progression.

David H Maxfield

Mormonism

Introduction

The members of *The Church of Jesus Christ of Latter-Day Saints,* or *LDS Church* are also known as *Mormons.* They get that nickname from the *Book of Mormon* which is one of their books of scripture.

The LDS Church claims a worldwide membership of over 12,000,000 with an aggressive program to convert people to their faith. The have over 70,000 full time missionaries in over 200 countries.

Origin

About 1830, Joseph Smith Jr. founded the LDS, or Mormon Church. The date is a little vague, but that is when the first edition of the Book of Mormon was published. The origin could be traced back to an earlier time when Smith, a young man at the age of 14 claimed to have received a series of visitations. In the first, he claimed he was praying for guidance as to which church to join, when he had a divine visitation and was told he should join none. There was not a church on earth acceptable to God, since the one true church, as established by Jesus, ceased to exist with the death of the apostles. Now, through Smith, the church and the priesthood were to be restored.

Book of Mormon.

Smith claimed he had another visitation from an angel who told him of a book that was like the Bible but included a record of the people who lived on the American continent. It was written on golden plates and had been hidden for centuries. He claimed to have retrieved these golden plates, and then translated them, without error, by inspiration from God.

Interestingly enough, Smith's translation of the Book of Mormon had many passages that were word for word as those found in the King James version, "KJV," of the Bible. Since the passages are attributed to different original authors, it creates doubt about the golden plates and causes speculation that they were just copied from the Bible. Small wonder that the KJV is the LDS Church's only accepted translation. Yet, even then, they leave themselves an excuse when one of their teachings is not consistent with the Bible.

Quoting their eighth article of faith:

"We believe the Bible to be the word of Good as far as it is translated correctly; we also believe the Book of Mormon to be the word of God.

It is important to pause here and consider what they really mean by that statement. They claim there was an error in translation whenever the Bible contradicts one of their teachings. However, that is just not so. Even now, scholars can refer back to the original manuscripts to determine if the Bible has been translated correctly. Many translations are available today that are easier for us to understand rather than the one written in the English in the time of King James. Anyway, where contradictions exist between Mormons and Christians, it is interpretation, not translation. Interpretation is the meaning one person might derive from a passage.

Included in the *Standard Works of the LDS Church* are the *Doctrine and Covenants* and *Pearl of Great Price*. They claim these also are without error because they believe Joseph Smith received direct revelation from God in writing or translating these books. However, as we shall see, the Pearl of Great Price has been discredited and there are contradictions between the Book of Mormon and the Doctrine and Covenants as well as between these books and the Bible.

Basic beliefs.

Mormons have some rather unique beliefs about God. They teach that our Father in heaven is Elohiym and is one of many Gods. They teach that Jesus is one of His spirit children and was formerly Jehovah, the God of the Old Testament. They also believe in the Holy Ghost. These three make up their Godhead that is further described as:

▶ The Father is a resurrected man who became a God.

▶ The Son is our elder spirit brother, who also took a body, lived, died, and was resurrected.

▶ The Holy Ghost, who unlike the Father and Son does not have a body but remains Spirit.

They teach that God was first a man like us, and they too may become Gods.

Quoting from Teachings of the Prophet Joseph Smith, pp. 345-46

> *"As man is, God once was, and as God is, man may become."*

> *"This is the way our heavenly Father became God."*
> *Joseph Smith taught: "It is the first principle of the*

Gospel to know for a certainty the character of God. ... He was once a man like us; . . . God himself, the Father of us all, dwelt on an earth, the same as Jesus Christ himself did."

This requires further examination. *God was once a man like us.* For most people it is incomprehensible to even imagine such a thing. That God, our maker and creator of the universe was once a man, who learned how to progress to become a God? Doesn't that make you want to ask, "If the Father of Jesus is God, and God has a Father, who is the Grandfather of Jesus? Beyond that, who is the Great-grandfather of them all?"

At the root of the question is: who came first, God or Man? Either you believe in a Creator who has always been God, or that a man evolved to become God. As you will see, the Bible has much to say about this. For example:

Ps 90:2

2 Before the mountains were brought forth,

Or ever You had formed the earth and the world,

Even from everlasting to everlasting, You are God. "NKJV"

Notice the present tense, "You are God," from everlasting to everlasting, or always.

Their own scriptures contradict their present concept of God.

Quoting from their Book of Mormon, this passage is quite different than what the Mormon Church teaches today.

Mosiah 15:1-5

1. God himself shall come down among the children of men and shall redeem his people. 2. And because he dwelleth in flesh he shall be called the Son of God and having subjected the flesh to the will of the Father, being the Father and the Son—3. The Father, because he was conceived by the power of God; and the Son, because of the flesh; thus becoming the Father and Son—4. And they are one God, yea, the very Eternal Father of heaven and of earth.

Their teachings about God have evolved over time. After the Book of Mormon was published in 1830, in their *Lectures of Faith*, published in 1835, Joseph Smith describes the Trinity as:

▶ The Father is spirit

▶ The Son is flesh

▶ The Holy Ghost (Holy Spirit) as the mind of the Father and Son

The story of the first vision has been changed many times over the years. However, even with the many changes in the Book of Mormon since its first printing, this passage in Mosiah remains in glaring opposition to their current beliefs about God.

The Bible also refutes their current teachings.

They teach that before Jesus was born, he was Jehovah, the God of Abraham, which is to say, the God of the Old Testament. However, according to the KJV of the Bible, Jesus was His Son.

Acts 3:13

13 The God of Abraham, and of Isaac, and of Jacob, the God of our fathers, hath glorified his Son Jesus; "KJV"

Therefore, we see contradictions between what the Mormon Church teaches today, within their own scriptures as well as the Bible. A quick review:

▶ Joseph Smith claimed to have translated the Book of Mormon from golden plates. Within it is the passage from Mosiah describing the Father as Spirit.

▶ Then he gave a similar description in the Lectures of Faith.

▶ These are in agreement with the passage in Acts from the Bible.

▶ Then Smith introduces their doctrine of *exaltation* "As man is, God once was, and as God is, man may become."

▶ Following that, the LDS Church incorporates the new concept of God into the official version of the first vision Smith claimed to have.

What should be painfully obvious is that Smith never claimed he had a visitation by two personages, the Father and Son, because at that time and long afterwards, he held a more Biblical belief. In fact, church records indicate several of those who followed in Smith's role, as proclaimed prophet, and president of the LDS Church, were undecided about the account of the first vision.

For my Mormon friends, contradictions and evolution of basic truths have nothing to do with revelation for different dispensations. God the Father is either spirit or was once a man like us. The Church teachings have changed, but He has not.

Was Jesus just our older spirit brother, or uniquely, the Son of God?

Just as they attempt to elevate man to become just like God, they reduce Jesus to be just like us. As their story goes, there was a pre-existence. Before we came to earth and took bodies of flesh and blood, we were first spirit children of our Father in heaven, Elohiym. At some point, there was a council of the Gods. They decided it was worthwhile, in our eternal progression, or ongoing education, to live as man. Lucifer, the brother of Jesus presented a plan. He would save all the people on earth, for his glory. Jesus said he would do all that was necessary for mankind to be saved, but everyone would have their own free will to accept the plan of salvation or reject it. This he would do for the glory of his Father. Continuing with the story, the plan of Jesus was accepted. Lucifer was cast out of heaven and one third of the heavenly hosts with him.

The Bible is clear on this.

In this passage, Jesus was speaking of himself and it shows how exceptional he is.

John 6:46

46 No one has seen the Father except the one who is from God; only he has seen the Father. "NIV"

Moreover, as we saw in the section for Jehovah's Witnesses, Satan is a fallen angel, and Jesus is not an angel. Additionally, the Bible contradicts the comparison of Jesus as our elder brother. In the previous verse, Jesus states that the Father sent him alone. In the following two verses, we see that no one else was sent. First, Jesus declares the difference between those born of women, and those in heaven.

> *Matt 11:11*
>
> *11 I tell you the truth: Among those born of women there has not risen anyone greater than John the Baptist; yet he who is least in the kingdom of heaven is greater than he. "NIV"*

Next, our spirits were formed within us. There was not any pre-existence.

> *Zech 12:1*
>
> *the LORD, who stretches out the heavens, who lays the foundation of the earth, and who forms the spirit of man within him, "NIV"*

Rather than being spirit children conceived by our Father in heaven, the Bible says that we can be adopted by Him. There is more on this later.

These are only some of the reasons why others who identify themselves as Christians disassociate themselves from Mormons. Probably the biggest reason is not their teachings on who Jesus is, but about what he has done for us.

Does it matter how we live our life?

For most people, the answer to this question is yes. However, for Mormons who are trying to achieve Godhood, the question goes deeper. They believe there are certain things that need to be accomplished in order to achieve the highest degree of glory and attain Godhood. Among them are temple ordinances, and you must be living according to the principles of the Church in order to get a temple recommend or permission to even enter the temple.

Actually, Mormons rely on good works for their salvation.

Quoting from the LDS, or Mormon, 3rd Article of Faith:

> *"We believe that through the atonement of Christ, all*

mankind may be saved, by obedience to the laws and ordinances of the Gospel."

To get a better understanding we need to break their statement into two parts.

"We believe that through the atonement of Christ, all mankind may be saved,"

They teach there is a *General Salvation* that has nothing to do with our personal sin. In essence, they believe that when Adam sinned that he and all of his descendants became subject to death. Christ died to pay the price for Adam's sin, and the gift of God is eternal life for everyone. As we saw with the Jehovah's Witnesses, and will be covered later in the section about God, if you only look at certain passages from the Bible, we can see where they get that idea.

Rom 5:18-20

18 Therefore, as through one man's offense judgment came to all men, resulting in condemnation, even so through one Man's righteous act the free gift came to all men, resulting in justification of life. 19 For as by one man's disobedience many were made sinners, so also by one Man's obedience many will be made righteous. "NKJV"

The problem is with the next part that continues with how we may be saved:

"by obedience to the laws and ordinances of the Gospel."

They teach there is an *Individual Salvation*, whereby mankind may secure a remission of personal sins by way of their own works. Those who have adhered to the commandments and completed the ordinances of the LDS or Mormon Church will continue to advance on their path toward *exaltation:* to become equal with God.

This is quite different from what we read in the Bible.

As we saw in the section about Jehovah's Witnesses, the Bible tells us that Christ died so that whoever believes should not perish. However, God's wrath remains on those who reject the son, and they will not have everlasting life.

> *John 3:36*
>
> *36 He who believes in the Son has everlasting life; and he who does not believe the Son shall not see life, but the wrath of God abides on him." "NKJV"*

We are not saved by obedience to laws.

> *Gal 2:16*
>
> *16 knowing that a man is not justified by the works of the law but by faith in Jesus Christ, even we have believed in Christ Jesus, that we might be justified by faith in Christ and not by the works of the law;* ***for by the works of the law no flesh shall be justified.*** *"NKJV"*

> *Gal 2:21*
>
> *21 I do not set aside the grace of God, for if righteousness could be gained through the law, Christ died for nothing!" "NIV"*

Nor are we saved by observing ordinances.

Rather, righteousness, apart from the laws and ordinances, comes by faith. In the following passage, Paul was clear about this. He begins by describing his own claim to be declared righteous and then discounts it as meaningless.

Phil 3:4-9

4 though I also might have confidence in the flesh. If anyone else thinks he may have confidence in the flesh, I more so: 5 circumcised the eighth day of the stock of Israel, of the tribe of Benjamin, a Hebrew of the Hebrews; concerning the law, a Pharisee; 6 concerning zeal, persecuting the church; concerning the righteousness which is in the law, blameless. 7 But what things were gain to me, these I have counted loss for Christ. 8 Yet indeed I also count all things loss for the excellence of the knowledge of Christ Jesus my Lord, for whom I have suffered the loss of all things, and count them as rubbish, that I may gain Christ 9 and be found in Him, not having my own righteousness, which is from the law, but that which is through faith in Christ, the righteousness which is from God by faith; "NKJV"

Paul could have been speaking directly to the Mormons when he said:

Gal 3:1-5

3:1 You foolish Galatians! (Mormons)! Who has bewitched you? Before your very eyes, Jesus Christ was clearly portrayed as crucified. 2 I would like to learn just one thing from you: Did you receive the Spirit by observing the law, or by believing what you heard? 3 Are you so foolish? After beginning with the Spirit, are you now trying to attain your goal by human effort? 4 Have you suffered so much for nothing-if it really was for nothing? 5 Does God give you his Spirit and work miracles among you because you observe the law, or because you believe what you heard? "NIV"

Through this passage, Paul was attempting to reach the people who once understood, placing their faith in the atonement of Christ. Now they were reverting to observing laws and ordinances in order to please God. These unfortunate people were willing to dedicate their lives to service but missed the message that God had sent to all of us.

As we have seen, this religion is based on obeying the laws and ordinances that they adhere to, but to believe that is what God requires for salvation is unbiblical.

We are saved by grace, or unmerited favor, if we place our faith in Jesus. That he who was without sin took our place on the cross to suffer and die to satisfy the law, so that we may go free. We are pardoned because he took the punishment that we deserve. Once free from the condemnation of our sinful lives, we are free to live a life that God will judge for commendation. There is more on this in the section about God.

What are they striving for?

The goal for Mormons is *exaltation:* to be equal with God.

Quoting from various Mormon sources and their scriptures:

> *We can become like our heavenly Father. This is exaltation. Our heavenly Father is perfect. However, he is not jealous of his wisdom and perfection. He glories in the fact that it is possible for his children to become like him. He has said,*

> *"This is my work and my glory--to bring to pass the immortality and eternal life of man" Book of Mormon, Moses 1:39*

> *"If we prove faithful to the Lord, we will live in the highest degree of the celestial kingdom of heaven. We will become exalted, just like our heavenly Father.*

Exaltation is the greatest gift that heavenly Father can give his children" Doctrine and Covenants, "D&C" 14:7.

They teach that exaltation comes through eternal progression.

That we will have everything that our heavenly Father and Jesus Christ have--all power, glory, dominion, and knowledge.

President Joseph Fielding Smith wrote: "The Father has promised through the Son that all that he has shall be given to those who are obedient to his commandments. They shall increase in knowledge, wisdom, and power, going from grace to grace, until the fullness of the perfect day shall burst upon them" Doctrines of Salvation, 2:36.

The Prophet Joseph Smith taught: "When you climb up a ladder, you must begin at the bottom, and ascend step by step, until you arrive at the top; and so it is with the principles of the Gospel--you must begin with the first and go on until you learn all the principles of exaltation. But it will be a great while after you have passed through the veil [died] before you will have learned them. It is not all to be comprehended in this world; it will be a great work to learn our salvation and exaltation even beyond the grave" Teachings of the Prophet Joseph Smith, p. 348.

What happens when we die?

They teach we will either continue on the path of eternal progression, or be damned, which prevents us from advancing.

What about heaven?

Mormons have some unique ideas about heaven. They believe that all but a few will go to heaven, but within heaven, there are three degrees of Glory.

- ▶ Celestial
- ▶ Telestial
- ▶ Terrestrial

They teach that even the lowest degree of heaven is better than anything we can imagine. The middle degree is for those who have lived a good life to the best of their ability and understanding, but the highest degree is reserved for Mormons.

In order to continue with one's exaltation, one must enter the Celestial realm of heaven. In order to do so, one must adhere to all the teachings of the LDS Church and complete certain ordinances. They refer to a passage in the Bible to validate this belief, but upon further examination, it is obvious that the Mormon Church has misinterpreted this passage.

> *1 Cor 15:40*
>
> *40 There are also celestial bodies, and bodies terrestrial: but the glory of the celestial is one, and the glory of the terrestrial is another. "KJV"*

As stated earlier, we can still refer to the original manuscripts that were written in Hebrew, Aramaic, and Greek. First, we will look at the definitions of these two words, and then look at another much-respected translation of this passage.

> *epouranios (ep-oo-ran'-ee-os); above the sky:*
>
> *KJV - celestial, (in) heaven (-ly), high.*
>
> *epigeios (ep-ig'-i-os); worldly (physically or morally):*

KJV - earthly, in earth, terrestrial.

Biblesoft's New Exhaustive Strong's Numbers and Concordance with Expanded Greek-Hebrew Dictionary. Copyright (c) 1994, Biblesoft and International Bible Translators, Inc.

Now let us look at the New International Version translation. See how it fits the definitions and clarifies that the author was trying to describe something entirely different. If you look in the greater context of this chapter, you will see he was using this as an illustration, not to reveal many heavens but to answer questions about the dead being raised to life.

1 Cor 15:35-42

35 But someone may ask, "How are the dead raised? With what kind of body will they come?" 36 How foolish! What you sow does not come to life unless it dies. 37 When you sow, you do not plant the body that will be, but just a seed, perhaps of wheat or of something else. 38 But God gives it a body as he has determined, and to each kind of seed, he gives its own body. 39 All flesh is not the same: Men have one kind of flesh, animals have another, birds another and fish another.

See how this verse makes much more sense in context and translated in the language of today from the original Greek.

40 There are also heavenly bodies and there are earthly bodies; but the splendor of the heavenly bodies is one kind, and the splendor of the earthly bodies is another.

41 The sun has one kind of splendor, the moon another and the stars another; and star differs from star in splendor. 42 So will it be with the resurrection of the dead. The body that is sown is perishable, it is raised imperishable; "NIV"

This is a good example of why it is important to read the verse before, the verse following, and in the context of the chapter, to gain the best understanding of any verse. Sometimes it is also necessary to view the chapter within the framework of the book, considering the author, to whom they were writing, and under what circumstances. Then view that within the perspective of the Bible as a whole.

What about hell?

According to Mormon doctrine, there are two hells. The first is where evil people go after death, but before their resurrection. They are punished for their sins, but not for eternity. They believe there is an end to this hell and at some point; everyone will eventually go to at least the lowest degree of heaven.

They do not believe that damnation is being cast into hell and eternal torment, but as being dammed like damming a river to stop the natural flow towards the otherwise natural outcome. In their case, it means stopping in your progression to become a God.

The second hell is described in the Bible as the lake of fire that burns forever. They would like to believe that this is reserved only for Satan, his angels and the sons of perdition, whose number you can count on the fingers of one hand.

However, hell is real, and you do not want to go there. There is more on this important point in the previous section on Jehovah's Witnesses.

What is the appeal?

On the surface, it has universal appeal. Our loving Father

in heaven desires that we have a loving relationship with our earthly families too. He promises that if we adhere to the teachings of the LDS Church, we will be sealed to our families for all time and eternity. Our benevolent Father in heaven wants us to progress and one day become just like Him. One day, to become Gods of our own worlds.

They have a prophet who leads the church by revelation from God.

What are some apparent problems with this set of beliefs?

We have already discussed some of the problems. Let us continue with refuting the basic premise that the church established by Jesus Christ ceased to exist with the death of the last of the original apostles.

Apostolic succession.

The Mormons claim the LDS Church is the only true church with all the power and authority of the priesthood. They base this on their belief that it was restored through Joseph Smith. This presupposes that the church established by Jesus Christ ceased to exist after the death of the original apostles.

However, the Roman Catholic and Eastern Orthodox Churches would disagree. They claim "apostolic succession" to this day. However, as we saw in the section on Roman Catholicism, this chain of authority is not necessary. We can have direct access to the Father through Jesus, who remains our high priest forever.

The foundation of the LDS Church.

If the LDS Church, the Mormons, rely on Joseph Smith as being a true prophet of God, then their whole belief system lives or dies with him. Like a house built of cards, it collapses when the foundation is removed. As we saw in the section on Jehovah's Witnesses, the Bible tells us we can determine if a prophet is true or not. We just observe if whether what they say will happen, happens.

Here are just a couple of examples of specific prophecies that were not fulfilled. The Book of Mormon declares that Jesus' birth was to take place in Jerusalem (Alma 7:9,10), whereas it actually took place in Bethlehem. Then in several places the Doctrine and Covenants asserts that western Missouri would be the site of "Zion" and a temple to the Lord would be built there within one generation of 1832, which did not happen.

Faced with no prophecies being fulfilled, the Mormons shift their focus to another definition for a prophet as one who receives revelations from God and speaks for Him. However, Joseph Smith fails that test too. Contradictions between their scriptures prove they are not inspired words of God. This is a major problem for the LDS Church.

When Smith introduced polygamy, he claimed that this was a "new and everlasting covenant" revealed to him by God. Yet, a short time later, upon pressure from the United States government, another leader of the LDS Church renounced polygamy. Obviously, God would not declare an "everlasting" covenant only to have it overturned by man.

Moreover, if the LDS Church claims Joseph Smith received direct revelation from God for the Doctrine and Covenants, and inspiration directly from God to translate the Book of Mormon, how could these be contradictory? Yet they are! For example:

Their Doctrine and Covenants says:

> *38: David also received many wives and concubines, and also Solomon and Moses my servants,... 39: David's*

wives and concubines were given unto him of me, by the hand of Nathan, my servant, saith the Lord. D&C 132:38,39.

Which is contradicted by their Book of Mormon that says:

For behold, thus saith the Lord: This people begin to wax in iniquity; they understand not the scriptures, for they seek to excuse themselves in committing whoredoms, because of the things which were written concerning David, and Solomon his son. Behold, David and Solomon truly had many wives and concubines, which thing was abominable before me, saith the Lord. BofM: Jacob 2:23-24

Obviously, the Lord would not call something He did an abomination.

The passage in the Book of Mormon predates the supposed revelation from God found in the Doctrine and Covenants. It states God gave David's many wives and concubines to him. Yet, the Doctrine and Covenants states that these things were an abomination! A few examples for synonyms of abomination are disgrace, outrage, scandal, or atrocity. You get the idea.

Therefore, since Joseph Smith, who claims to have translated the Book of Mormon, without error, as a direct revelation from God, and his words are recorded in the Doctrine and Covenants as revelations from God, he does not meet the standard for a prophet according to the Bible. Moreover, it brings all of his teachings into question.

Their *Pearl of Great Price* also lacks credibility.

The second part of the *Pearl Great Price* contains the *Book of Abraham*. It was supposed to have been written on Egyptian papyrus by Abraham himself about 4,000 years ago, which in itself would be quite incredible. According to Mormon officials, this same papyrus fell into Joseph Smith's hands and he began translating it in 1835.

For many years, Joseph Smith's collection of papyri was lost and there was no way to check the accuracy of his translation. On Nov. 27, 1967, however, the Mormon-owned *Deseret News* made the startling announcement that the collection had been rediscovered in the Metropolitan Museum of Art. The newspaper article went on to say: "Included in the papyri is a manuscript identified as the original document from which Joseph Smith had copied the drawing which he called 'Facsimile No. 1' and published with the Book of Abraham."

The importance of this find cannot be overemphasized; it, in fact, made it possible to put Joseph Smith's ability as a translator of ancient Egyptian writing to an absolute test. Within six months from the time the Metropolitan Museum gave the papyri to the church, the Book of Abraham had been proven untrue! The fall of the Book of Abraham was brought about by the identification of the actual piece of papyrus from which Joseph Smith claimed to "translate" the book.

The identification of this fragment as the original from which Joseph Smith claimed to translate the Book of Abraham has been made possible by a comparison with Joseph Smith's *Egyptian Alphabet and Grammar* (available at www.utlm.org), handwritten documents by Joseph Smith's scribes which were photographically reproduced in 1966.

Noted Egyptologists Richard A. Parker and Klaus Baer and others have translated this papyrus fragment and found that it is in reality the *Egyptian Book of Breathings*. Even the Mormon apologist Hugh Nibley has admitted this identification. In fact, he has even made his own translation of the text.

It is obvious; therefore, that the papyrus Joseph Smith claimed was the Book of Abraham is in reality an Egyptian funerary text known as the Book of Breathings. It is a pagan document, filled with magical practices and the names of Egyptian gods and goddesses. It has absolutely nothing to do with either Abraham or his religion.

As a note to my Mormon friends, these things are *not* subject to interpretation. This is not looking at certain passages in the Bible from different perspectives. These are verifiable problems with what the Mormon Church teaches that cannot just be dismissed. Rather than listen to man, seek to understand what God says. He is not the author of confusion.

What does the Bible tell us?

In the first place, contrary to how the LDS Church portrays different Gods, the Bible as revealed in the original Hebrew text combines Elohiym with Yehovah, from the original Hebrew, YHVH, translated Jehovah. It is a different reference to God, not different God's. To make it easier to follow, I have included the entire passage, followed by clarification using *Strong's* translation from the original text.

> *Ex 6:7-8*
>
> *7 I will take you as My people, and I will be your God. Then you shall know that I am the LORD your God who brings you out from under the burdens of the Egyptians. 8 And I will bring you into the land which I swore to give to Abraham, Isaac, and Jacob; and I will give it to you as a heritage: I am the LORD.' "NKJV"*

In the original Hebrew, the word for God here, is "elohiym."

> *OT:430*
>
> *'elohiym (el-o-heem'); plural of OT: 433; gods*

in the ordinary sense; but specifically used (in the plural thus, especially with the article) of the supreme God; occasionally applied by way of deference to magistrates; and sometimes as a superlative:

(Biblesoft's New Exhaustive Strong's Numbers and Concordance with Expanded Greek-Hebrew Dictionary. Copyright (c) 1994, Biblesoft and International Bible Translators, Inc.)

The passage continues declaring I am the LORD, *Yehovah*.

OT: 3068

Yehovah (yeh-ho-vaw'); from OT: 1961; (the) self-Existent or Eternal; Jehovah, Jewish national name of God:

(Biblesoft's New Exhaustive Strong's Numbers and Concordance with Expanded Greek-Hebrew Dictionary. Copyright (c) 1994, Biblesoft and International Bible Translators, Inc.)

As shown earlier, elohiym is descriptive of the trinity, or the plurality of God. One God who reveals Himself in three persons and in another context, describes him as one who judges.

The Bible says there are no other Gods, nor will there ever be.

Replacing the same words for LORD with Yehovah and God with elohiym, the Bible interchanges these words while declaring there is one God.

Isa 43:10-11

10 "You are My witnesses," says the LORD," And My servant whom I have chosen, That you may know and believe Me, And understand that I am He.

Before Me there was no God formed, Nor shall there be after Me. 11 I, even I, am the LORD, And besides Me there is no savior. "NKJV"

Isa 44:6

6 "Thus says the LORD, the King of Israel, And his Redeemer, the LORD of hosts: 'I am the First and I am the Last; Besides Me there is no God. "NKJV"

Isa 45:18

18 For thus says the LORD, Who created the heavens, Who is God, Who formed the earth and made it, Who has established it, Who did not create it in vain, Who formed it to be inhabited: "I am the LORD, and there is no other. "NKJV"

The Bible warns that it is dangerous to believe that you can become like God.

Satan, Lucifer, the devil, was cast out of heaven because he said he would become like God.

Isa 14:12-14

12 "How you are fallen from heaven, O Lucifer, son of the morning!

How you are cut down to the ground, You who weakened the nations!

13 For you have said in your heart: 'I will ascend into heaven,

I will exalt my throne above the stars of God; I will also sit on the mount of the congregation On the farthest sides of the north; 14 I will ascend above the heights of the clouds, I will be like the Most High.' "NKJV"

What about heaven and hell?

Mormons have some unique ideas about heaven and hell. They believe that there is an end to hell. It is where wicked spirits go between death and resurrection. In one sense, it could be likened to purgatory as the Catholics teach. It makes you feel like God will judge us, but not too harshly. After we pay the penalty for our sins, we can enter heaven. However, that is not biblical.

The Bible warns us that hell is real, and we should fear it!

As we saw in the section devoted to Jehovah's Witlessness:

▶ The unsaved go there.

▶ People are conscious.

▶ Their senses suffer. They are in agony.

▶ They have a memory with mental and emotional regrets.

▶ There is not a second chance or communication with the living to warn and motivate others to repent.

▶ It is a place of punishment.

▶ It is a terrible place for all eternity.

You do not want to go there, and you do not want your friends to go there either.

And about heaven, the Bible warns, it is for the few, not the many.

As the previous chart, "Where are you in relationship to God?" illustrates:

Matt 7:13-15

13 "Enter through the narrow gate. For wide is the gate and broad is the road that leads to destruction, and many enter through it. 14 But small is the gate and narrow the road that leads to life, and only a few find it. 15 "Watch out for false prophets. "NIV"

Where you place your trust has eternal consequences.

It is the most important decision you will ever make.

The Mormon Church teaches that Christ died so that all who ever lived will be resurrected. All except for a handful of people, known as the sons of perdition, will go to heaven, and there we will be judged for how we lived our lives. Those who obey all the laws, and observe the ordinances of the LDS Church, will have the opportunity to progress throughout eternity to become just like God.

However, these teachings are not Biblical. Not everyone will be admitted to heaven and hell is real. There is one judgment for condemnation and another for commendation. Only those who have passed the first judgment will be rewarded by the second. This is discussed in detail in the section on God.

Hinduism

Introduction

The origin of Hinduism can be traced to India where it still makes up about 80% of the population. What is more difficult is to identify any particular person as originator of this belief system.

It began about 1500 BC as a polytheistic and ritualistic religion. Over time, the rituals grew in number and became more complex. Between about 800 and 300 BC, they were recorded in writings known as the *Upanishads*.

Typical of other belief systems, the priests who performed the rituals gained power and control over the adherents and enjoyed more privileges. The ritualism took on more prominence until about 600 BC, when many moved away from ritualism to meditation. A comparison could be made to divisions in other belief systems. Some place their trust in the authority of a priest or other prominent figure, while others place more emphasis on what they consider to be sacred writings for guidance or practices like meditation.

It has been estimated that approximately 13% of the world's population identify themselves as Hindu. There are over a billion, with over 850,000,000 in India alone.

Far beyond the number of Hindus is the number of other people who have been influenced by Hinduism in one form or another. Some of those influenced are Buddhists; the mind science groups like Christian Science; New Age groups like those practicing meditation; and other philosophical religions or belief systems.

Basic beliefs

Hinduism is actually remarkably diverse. In fact, it might be better described as a culture rather than a religion or philosophy. The practices and beliefs not only differ from country to country, or region, but even from family to family. This is largely because it tends to be all-inclusive. Not just tolerant of other faiths, Hinduism tends to embrace other faiths, sometimes incorporating other beliefs into Hinduism.

Hinduism can be described as *Henotheistic*, meaning worshiping one God without denying the existence of other gods. They believe in many manifestations of *Brahman*, the one Supreme Being. According to Hinduism, Brahman is an impersonal, unapproachable force of existence without attributes; therefore, Brahman is incapable of having a relationship with us. Yet, with its diversity, we can identify some doctrines that seem consistent throughout all sects of Hinduism.

Brahma

The impersonal life force within all things; "god." (Pantheism)

Karma

Karma could be described as "What goes around comes around" or "cause and effect." Evil will be repaid by evil, and good will be repaid with reward. If you do well in this life, you will be rewarded and may advance toward the ultimate goal of nirvana. Conversely, those who do not do well will be punished, or work off their bad karma, or be destined to do it all over again until the lessons of this life are learned.

Reincarnation

The concept of reincarnation is the result of believing in karma. Reincarnation is a cycle of birth, life, death, and rebirth. To the Hindu, it may mean being reborn as a human, animal, or insect. We are reincarnated until we reach nirvana.

Nirvana

Nirvana is achieving oneness with Brahma or becoming united with God. (Monism)

Does it matter how we live our life?

You can work off bad karma. Nevertheless, according to the *caste* system, you should not try to advance from one caste to another within one's lifetime. Otherwise, when reincarnated, you will have to go through that caste again in order to learn the lessons of life you should have been learning.

What are they striving for?

Moksha, deliverance from the endless cycle of life, death, reincarnation, and union with Brahma. There are three paths to moksha.

One is by works, or *dharma.* The second, a more difficult way, is through knowledge, or *inana.* The third is a passionate devotion to a god, with any god being acceptable. It could be one of the many gods, goddesses, or demigods in the Hindu pantheon.

What happens when we die?

Reincarnation, until through moksha, you break the cycle.

What is the appeal?

The appeal may be its philosophy that many paths lead to God. Therefore, allowing you to believe what you will, or follow your heart and still find God.

On the other hand, it may be that it seems to offer a way to escape from suffering. If you live this life to the best of your ability, within your station or caste, ultimately you can break out of the cycle of reincarnation and suffering.

My guess is that you would not convert to Hinduism; you were probably born into it. This is an unhappy lifestyle. Unlike others who believe that reincarnation means you keep getting another chance until you get it right, with the caste system you have no chance in this life, and since life is all about suffering, your goal is to break the cycle of *samsara,* or reincarnation.

What are some apparent problems with this set of beliefs?

It did not start with anyone claiming a revelation from God, nor anything close. The foundation of Hinduism is unknown. Who came up with the caste system? The idea of karma and reincarnation? Anyone could have dreamt them up. Let us speculate on the evolution of this belief system.

The caste system.

If we take a critical look at the structure, it appears it was devised to control people. In the first position, we have the Brahmins, or priests of Brahma. We might conclude that these Brahmins created the caste system since they enjoyed a lot of power, authority and now with the caste system, the highest position.

Just under them were the warriors and nobles. This makes sense, since those who seek power want to protect their position; they give second place to the defenders.

Below that were the merchants, then slaves and finally the untouchables. That would appeal to the merchants who had slaves, and even the slaves would feel good about themselves knowing there was a caste below them.

Karma

Obviously, what goes around does not come around. Anyone can see that life is not fair. People are not always rewarded or punished for their behavior. Therefore, somewhere along the way, someone introduced the idea of reincarnation.

Reincarnation

Reincarnation is a concept that appears to have come about through circular reasoning.

Circular reasoning.

Circular reasoning is the process of viewing the facts in light of your forgone conclusion. This is what happens when you first believe something to be true and then adjust the information so that it agrees with your forgone conclusion.

In this case, people realized that karma does not happen in one lifetime. Therefore, if you start out with a belief in karma, in order to validate your belief you use circular reasoning. For example, if I believe "x," and "x" is not so, then I believe "y" to validate "x" anyway. If I can see that karma, "x," doesn't seem to be true in my life, then, "y," it must be true in my next life. If you believe something is true or want it to be true, people find ways to make it true. In this case, x = karma, and y = reincarnation.

No forgiveness of sins.

We are just on the treadmill of life, death, and reincarnation.

Maybe the problem for Hinduism is that it is a compilation of conflicting ideas. Rather than seeking the truth, they remain confused and have concluded that all paths lead to God.

What does the Bible tell us?

There is one God, who wants us to know Him, and the truth.

> *1 Cor 14:33*
>
> *33 For God is not a God of confusion but of peace. "RSV"*

If you look at the root appeal of reincarnation, it is like forgiving ourselves. We recognize our shortcomings. We may not get it right, but we will have repeated chances until we do. However, the Bible refutes that.

> *Heb 9:27*
>
> *27 Just as man is destined to die once, and after that to face judgment, "NIV"*

No second chance.

We only have one chance to get it right. Either live a life acceptable to God, or face condemnation.

> *John 5:28-29*
>
> *28 "Do not be amazed at this, for a time is coming when all who are in their graves will hear his voice 29 and come out-those who have done good will rise to live, and those who have done evil will rise to be condemned. "NIV"*

Evidenced by the physical resurrection of Jesus.

On the third day after Jesus died, he was resurrected, not reincarnated. He was alive and had a body of flesh and bones.

Luke 24:36-43

36 And while they were telling these things, He Himself stood in their midst. 37 But they were startled and frightened and thought that they were seeing a spirit. 38 And He said to them, "Why are you troubled, and why do doubts arise in your hearts? 39 "See My hands and My feet, that it is I Myself; touch Me and see, for a spirit does not have flesh and bones as you see that I have." 40[And when He had said this, He showed them His hands and His feet.] 41 And while they still could not believe it for joy and were marveling, He said to them, "Have you anything here to eat?" 42 And they gave Him a piece of a broiled fish; 43 and He took it and ate it before them. "NAS"

Jesus rose from the dead with the same body he had when put to death. He showed his followers the wounds of the nails driven through his hands and feet, and the sword that had pierced his side.

John 20:24-29

24 But Thomas, one of the twelve, called Didymus, was not with them when Jesus came. 25 The other disciples therefore were saying to him, "We have seen the Lord!" But he said to them, "Unless I shall see in His hands the imprint of the nails and put my finger into the place of the nails, and put my hand into His side, I will not believe."

26 And after eight days again His disciples were inside, and Thomas with them. Jesus came, the doors having been shut, and stood in their midst, and said, "Peace be with you." 27 Then He said to Thomas, "Reach here your finger, and see My hands; and reach here your hand, and put it into My side; and be not

> *unbelieving, but believing." 28 Thomas answered and said to Him, "My Lord and my God!" 29 Jesus said to him, "Because you have seen Me, have you believed? Blessed are they who did not see, and yet believed." "NAS"*

If you have ever heard the phrase "doubting Thomas," now you know where it comes from. Nevertheless, take note, blessed are those who believe by faith.

Jesus was not the only one to be resurrected.

Many people who had died had a physical resurrection, disproving reincarnation.

> *Matt 27:52-53*
>
> *52 The tombs broke open and the bodies of many holy people who had died were raised to life. 53 They came out of the tombs, and after Jesus' resurrection they went into the holy city and appeared to many people. "NIV"*

All we have is one lifetime to get things right.

However, one lifetime is all it takes. Moksha is not necessary, if we have forgiveness. There is much more on this throughout this book. In addition, there is incredibly good news. God loves us and has revealed Himself to us because He wants to have a relationship with us. He has even provided us with a spiritual guide, the Holy Spirit, to help us on our journey.

We can have a relationship with God, here and now, as well as hereafter.

There is more on this in the sections on Buddhism and Confucianism as well as the section about God.

Section III

Those believing they are God or can become God-like

There are many that fit into this section, thinking there is a little God in all of us, or that God is in everything. Then others might believe in God, but are so far from knowing, let alone worshiping Him that they are also included here. To gain a better understanding let us begin with some definitions used to describe certain beliefs.

Monism: **God is an impersonal oneness, or all is one.**

Two distinct groups fall into this category. Those that believe their inner being combined with everyone else makes up the fundamental nature of God. Then there are those who believe that one day they will become one in essence with God.

In either case, sin is irrelevant. Either believing that, "Since God is in all of us, I cannot sin." Or, "Since life is just a learning experience toward becoming more Godlike, it really doesn't matter if I make mistakes along the way. Eventually I will make the grade, becoming one with God." Whichever way has an appeal. Either I am God or will be one day. We will look at a couple of examples, followed by a look at Shinto, which is a good example of pantheism.

Pantheism: **God is All**

Pantheism (Greek: pan = all and Theos = God) literally means, "God is All" and "All is God." God is everything and everything is God, including the forces and workings of nature.

Christian Science

Introduction

Christian Science is one of the leading *Mind Science* religions. However, contrary to what the name implies, it has little to do with being a follower of Christ.

Mary Baker Eddy, 1821-1910, was the founder, but she was apparently influenced by Phineas Parker Quimby's teachings about mental-psychic healing. Her book, *Science and Health with Key to the Scriptures,* is used by Christian Scientists as a guide to interpret the Bible. She claimed it was the final revelation of God to mankind and asserted that her work was inspired of God. The word "Key" in the title of her book is in reference to her being the woman of Revelation 12; that she is the key to unlocking the Bible, which she called a dark book. She claimed the Bible had many mistakes and that her writings provided the key spoken of in Rev. 3:7.

In 1879, four years after the first publication of *Science and Health*, Mary Baker Eddy and some of her students voted to organize the *Church of Christ, Scientist* in Boston, Massachusetts. Of course, like all cults, it claimed to be the restoration of the original New Testament Church.

Basic beliefs

Like others, they say they believe the Bible, but that it is full of errors. In addition, there are secondary meanings hidden in the text. Therefore, the best way to ascertain the truth is to use her book as a companion guide. Sound familiar? It should, since we see similar pattern with Muslims, Jehovah's Witnesses and Mormons, to name a few.

They believe that God is impersonal, an all-encompassing spirit that is in everyone. We are all part of God.

What are they striving for?

The point of life is to achieve a certain state of mind. We need to come to the realization that life is an illusion. Nothing is real except mind or spirit. Matter is evil. Later in the book, you will be able to see the influence Buddhism had on this religion.

What is the appeal?

They can find the power to heal within themselves. Sin, sickness, and death are all illusions that can be overcome by correct thinking.

They do not believe they are subject to God. Christian Scientists view heaven, hell, and sin as irrelevant.

What are some apparent problems with this set of beliefs?

If psychic healing worked, and you were supposed to be part of God, why wouldn't it be successful every time? Having a healthy attitude promotes healing, but you are not really in control, otherwise, why isn't the world filled with healthy Christian Scientists?

This religion has nothing to do with God. Their concept of psychic healing has everything to do with self.

What does the Bible tell us?

There are many miraculous healings reported in the Bible. Jesus healed people who were blind or crippled since birth. He even raised people from the dead. More about these miracles will be discussed later. For now, let us focus on how God revealed Himself because people have been perplexed since the beginning of time.

You are not God, "I AM," declares the LORD!

God, in His infinite wisdom knew that we would be confused. He selected one man, Abraham, to reveal Himself to us. Abraham had faith, and it was accounted to him for righteousness. God promised Abraham that through him and his descendants, many would be blessed. The chain of events began with God revealing Himself to Abraham, then to his descendants, and through them, to the rest of us. We should all recognize the one true God by how he interacted with the descendants of Abraham. He started with a plan to gain their attention.

First God prepared the people. Fulfilling prophecy, after 400 years of bondage in Egypt, they were looking for a savior. Next God revealed himself to Moses and directed him to lead the people.

> *Ex 3:4-15*
>
> *4 When the LORD saw that he had gone over to look, God called to him from within the bush, "Moses! Moses!" And Moses said, "Here I am." 5 "Do not come any closer," God said. "Take off your sandals, for the place where you are standing is holy ground."*

> *6 Then he said, "I am the God of your father, the God of Abraham, the God of Isaac and the God of Jacob." At this, Moses hid his face, because he was afraid to look at God. 7 The LORD said, "I have indeed seen the misery of my people in Egypt. I have heard them crying out because of their slave drivers, and I am concerned about their suffering. 8 So I have come down to rescue them from the hand of the Egyptians and to bring them up out of that land into a good and spacious land, a land flowing with milk and honey-*
>
> *9 And now the cry of the Israelites has reached me, and I have seen the way the Egyptians are oppressing them. 10 So now, go. I am sending you to Pharaoh to bring my people the Israelites out of Egypt."*

He had identified Himself as the God of Abraham, as such, revealing Himself to the world.

> *11 But Moses said to God, "Who am I, that I should go to Pharaoh and bring the Israelites out of Egypt?" 12 And God said, "I will be with you. And this will be the sign to you that it is I who have sent you: When you have brought the people out of Egypt, you will worship God on this mountain." 13 Moses said to God, "Suppose I go to the Israelites and say to them, 'The God of your fathers has sent me to you,' and they ask me, 'What is his name?' Then what shall I tell them?" 14 God said to Moses, "I AM WHO I AM. This is what you are to say to the Israelites: 'I AM has sent me to you.'" 15 God also said to Moses, "Say to the Israelites, 'The LORD, the God of your fathers--the God of Abraham, the God of Isaac and the God of Jacob--has sent me to you.' This is my name forever, the name by which I am to be remembered from generation to generation. "NIV"*

Now we have the key to the beginning of understanding God. "I AM" is not a name! God was declaring, "I AM GOD." There is no need for a name because there is no other God. Moreover, as we saw in Mormonism, nor will there ever be any other God.

David H Maxfield

Church of Scientology

Introduction

The founder of Scientology was L. Ron Hubbard, 1911-1986, a successful science fiction writer. His book, *Dianetics: The Modern Science of Mental Health,* is the basis of this belief system.

There are relatively few adherents scattered around the world. It gets more notoriety because of the prominence of a few Hollywood stars who have embraced it.

Basic beliefs

Scientology promotes a belief in an extraterrestrial race called *Thetans.*

God as such is irrelevant since collectively, we all make up the essence of god, (Monism).

Does it matter how we live our life?

People are essentially good, but we must be reincarnated until the god-like Thetan status is realized. Through human reasoning, we can produce perfect behavior. Here again, sin is not a factor.

What is the appeal?

As you realize your Thetan origin, you see yourself as a

superior being. If not perfect yet, you are on the path, and one day you will be. You have the power within yourself to overcome your circumstances.

What are some apparent problems with this set of beliefs?

Founded by a science fiction writer, Scientology has no basis in fact. In contrast, the Bible teaches us that there is one, knowable God, and there is no reincarnation.

No reincarnation.

The following passage combined with those we looked at in the section on Hinduism; give further evidence that invalidates any belief in reincarnation.

> *1 Cor 15: 3-57 (not all inclusive, but focusing on the message)*
>
> *3 For what I received I passed on to you as of first importance: that Christ died for our sins according to the Scriptures, 4 that he was buried, that he was raised on the third day according to the Scriptures,*

An important side note, the references "according to Scriptures" are prophecy fulfilled, giving further evidence to support the Bible.

> *5 and that he appeared to Peter, and then to the Twelve. 6 After that, he appeared to more than five hundred of the brothers at the same time, most of whom are still living, though some have fallen asleep. 7 Then he appeared to James, then to all the apostles, 8 and last of all he appeared to me also, as to one abnormally born.*

Note that Paul pointed out that there were as many as five

hundred at one time who saw the resurrected Jesus. By the way, at the time this was written, they did not count the women and children who were present, so the number could have been much larger. Of greater importance, the people who were witnesses were not just his inner circle. These were ordinary people and Paul points out that many were still alive so that skeptics could verify what he was telling them.

> *9 For I am the least of the apostles and do not even deserve to be called an apostle, because I persecuted the church of God.*

Another noteworthy point is that Paul was not one of the original followers of Jesus. In fact, he persecuted the early church. He stood by as many earlier believers were put to death; all the time, thinking he was serving God. He came to a saving faith in Jesus after a miraculous experience. Continuing later in the passage:

> *14 And if Christ has not been raised, our preaching is useless and so is your faith. 15 More than that, we are then found to be false witnesses about God, for we have testified about God that he raised Christ from the dead.*

> *20 But Christ has indeed been raised from the dead, the firstfruits of those who have fallen asleep. 21 For since death came through a man, the resurrection of the dead comes also through a man. 22 For as in Adam all die, so in Christ all will be made alive.*

> *35 But someone may ask, "How are the dead raised? With what kind of body will they come?"*

Scripture tells us that when we are resurrected, we have a different kind of body. We will not grow old, nor see decay. Moreover, there will be no infirmities.

42 So will it be with the resurrection of the dead. The body that is sown is perishable, it is raised imperishable; 43 it is sown in dishonor, it is raised in glory; it is sown in weakness, it is raised in power; 44 it is sown a natural body, it is raised a spiritual body. If there is a natural body, there is also a spiritual body.

54 When the perishable has been clothed with the imperishable, and the mortal with immortality, then the saying that is written will come true: "Death has been swallowed up in victory."

55 "Where, O death, is your victory? Where, O death, is your sting?" 56 The sting of death is sin, and the power of sin is the law. 57 But thanks be to God! He gives us the victory through our Lord Jesus Christ. "NIV"

Conclusion: reincarnation is a myth. We die once, and then we are resurrected to face judgment. We do not get a second, thirtieth, or one-hundredth chance to get it right. The concept of reincarnation has its roots in Hinduism. As we saw in that section, the theory was developed through circular reasoning.

That may seem like bad news for those who like the idea that if they fall short of God's standards, they will have more lifetimes to get it right. However, the good news is that we do not have to become like God, because He became like us. There is more on this throughout this book including the section about God.

Shinto

Introduction

There was no real founder. It can be traced back to about 500 BC to what began as a collection fertility cults and nature worshipers. It was centered on *kami,* the belief that gods inhabited objects of nature, even rocks. (Pantheism)

As time went on, Buddhism, Taoism and Confucianism, which had come to Japan from China, influenced Shinto. In fact, the name *Shinto* is from the Chinese, "shin tao," or "way of the gods."

As with many religious groups, the number of followers is hard to determine. Some put the number at 3 million. Other estimates are that about 40% of Japanese adults follow Shinto, which would make the number many times larger. If you include those who have blended beliefs in Shinto and Buddhism, the number could go as high as 100 million or more.

Basic beliefs

While Shinto has many gods, it does not have a concept of a Creator. Interestingly, they seem to worship the creation, but not the Creator!

Something else that seems odd. While believing that the gods inhabit creation, they do not believe humans have a *soul,* or eternal nature.

As a parallel to Hinduism, they have priests who place a great deal of importance on practicing rituals. However, they do not have any sacred texts, or seeming relationship with God.

Does it matter how we live our life?

It seems that human behavior is more important than the involvement with any god.

Their concept of sin may be that of doing unacceptable behavior. In order to achieve harmony, one must recognize their poor behavior, and change their ways.

What are they striving for?

Shinto focuses more on the here and now. Moral behavior is the most important thing in life to them.

What happens when we die?

There is not really an afterlife, but being influenced by other religions, they have adopted the concept of nirvana. In their case, this means progressing into higher levels of knowledge through various life cycles.

What is the appeal?

A reverence for the creation has an appeal. However, it is not like people convert to Shinto. Typically, they were born into it as a matter of geography and history.

What are some apparent problems with this set of beliefs?

Instead of worshiping the Creator, they revere the creation.

What does the Bible tell us?

It is because of the creation that we should have adoration for the Creator.

Rom 1:21-23

21 For although they knew God, they neither glorified him as God nor gave thanks to him, but their thinking became futile and their foolish hearts were darkened. 22 Although they claimed to be wise, they became fools 23 and exchanged the glory of the immortal God for images made to look like mortal man and birds and animals and reptiles. "NIV"

For my friends who have been brought up in the culture of Shinto, God wants a relationship with you. He has revealed Himself through the creation and expects you to acknowledge and worship Him. This section is very brief, but there is more on this in the section about God.

Other Beliefs

Let us explore some groups that may take on one or more of these characteristics. What we usually find is a blend of thought, either acknowledged or not, by the followers. For example, people who believe in reincarnation and karma can trace the roots of this belief back to Hinduism. The Buddha was a Hindu before he became "enlightened." Buddhism spread to other countries like Japan and blended with their cultural adherence to Shinto. The practitioners of Shinto differ in their beliefs, yet in Japan, a Shinto priest may perform a wedding and a Buddhist monk may preside over a funeral.

Cross Cultural

The introduction of the Eastern belief systems to the West was around the 1960's beginning with the popular musical group, the Beatles. Since then, mysticism, the occult, and magic have had a considerable effect on American pop culture. Music, books, movies, and television have also been greatly influenced, which in turn, have influenced a large number of people.

New Age

The New Age movement is more a collection of beliefs but without an organization of believers. The term comes from a belief in astronomy, and that the new age of Aquarius will be a 2,000-year period of self-discovery, spiritual growth, and enlightenment. Furthermore, they are eclectic, drawing on the beliefs of many.

The occult, sorcery, and witchcraft:

The word occult comes from the Latin word *occultus* and literally means hidden, secret, or concealed. It is frequently used in reference to certain practices, including divination, fortune telling, spiritism and magic. There have been many books, movies and television shows romanticizing the supernatural. Many think it would be fun to know the future. What if we could even control the outcome? How about contacting the dead, or seeking spiritual advisors? We can imagine how all this could have an appeal. However, what if, in order to do these things, it means doing business with the devil?

What does the Bible say?

The Bible acknowledges the supernatural and warns us about it.

Deut 18:10-12

10 Let no one be found among you who sacrifices his son or daughter in the fire, who practices divination or sorcery, interprets omens, engages in witchcraft, 11 or casts spells, or who is a medium or spiritist or who consults the dead. 12 Anyone who does these things is detestable to the LORD. "NIV (also 2 Chron 33:6)

God is jealous and wants a relationship with us.

In the following account, Saul had been given a choice. He could seek guidance and obey the LORD, or more or less, do his own thing. He chose unwisely and it had dire consequences.

1 Chron 10:13-14

13 Saul died because he was unfaithful to the LORD; he did not keep the word of the LORD and even consulted a medium for guidance, 14 and did not inquire of the

> LORD. So the LORD put him to death and turned the kingdom over to David son of Jesse. "NIV"

> Clearly, God wants to be our spiritual guide. However, the choice is ours. In this instance, we can seek Him, attempting to do His will, or do our own thing by turning to the supernatural. If we deny Him, it has consequences both here and hereafter. We are not just talking about our physical death, but eternal punishment.

As we are warned in the following passage and elsewhere in this book, we should have a healthy fear of Satan, or the devil.

> *1Pe 5:8*

> *8 Be alert and of sober mind. Your enemy the devil prowls around like a roaring lion looking for someone to devour. "NIV"*

The truth is, even the demons acknowledge that there is one God over all.

Demons fear God

> *James 2:19*

> *19 You believe that there is one God. Good! Even the demons believe that-and shudder. "NIV"*

Demons acknowledge that Jesus is the Christ, the Son of God.

> *Luke 4:41*

> *41 Moreover, demons came out of many people, shouting, "You are the Son of God!" But he rebuked them and would not allow them to speak, because they knew he was the Christ. "NIV"*

Demons know that Jesus is the Holy One of God.

Mark 1:23-24

23 Just then a man in their synagogue who was possessed by an evil spirit cried out, 24 "What do you want with us, Jesus of Nazareth? Have you come to destroy us? I know who you are-the Holy One of God!" "NIV"

Demons believe in the deity of Jesus.

Mark 3:11

11 Whenever the evil spirits saw him, they fell down before him and cried out, "You are the Son of God." "NIV"

Demons believe an eternal punishment for sin is coming.

Luke 8:27-28

27 When Jesus stepped ashore, he was met by a demon-possessed man from the town. For a long time this man had not worn clothes or lived in a house, but had lived in the tombs. 28 When he saw Jesus, he cried out and fell at his feet, shouting at the top of his voice, "What do you want with me, Jesus, Son of the Most High God? I beg you, don't torture me!" "NIV"

Matt 8:28-29

28 When he arrived at the other side in the region of the Gadarenes, two demon-possessed men coming from the tombs met him. They were so violent that no one could pass that way. 29 "What do you want with us, Son of God?" they shouted. "Have you come here to torture us before the appointed time?" "NIV"

Be aware! There is a spiritual battle going on for our souls.

Satan uses many tactics to lead us astray and separate us from God.

2 Cor 4:3-4

3 And even if our gospel is veiled, it is veiled to those who are perishing. 4 The god of this age has blinded the minds of unbelievers, so that they cannot see the light of the gospel of the glory of Christ, who is the image of God. "NIV"

Be on guard! Satan will deceive many.

Speaking of the end times, the Bible forewarns us there will be signs and wonders by Satan and his servants.

2 Thess 2:8-12

8 Then this wicked one will appear, whom the Lord Jesus will burn up with the breath of his mouth and destroy by his presence when he returns. 9 This man of sin will come as Satan's tool, full of satanic power, and will trick everyone with strange demonstrations, and will do great miracles. 10 He will completely fool those who are on their way to hell because they have said no to the Truth; they have refused to believe it and love it and let it save them, 11 so God will allow them to believe lies with all their hearts, 12 and all of them will be justly judged for believing falsehood, refusing the Truth, and enjoying their sins. "TLB"

Fortunately, we have the Bible to refer to for the truth.

The Bible is clear about who God is, His nature, our relationship to Him, and the relationship He wants with us.

▶ We are not part of Him, nor will we ever become one with Him.

▶ He is holy and pure; we separate ourselves from Him by our sins.

▶ He will judge us by His standards, not ours.

▶ He has emotions such as love, anger, and compassion.

▶ He is jealous.

▶ He wants a relationship with us.

▶ If we reject Him, we face severe consequences.

While acknowledging there is a spirit world, we must understand that there is a battle going on between good and evil. According to the Bible, with God's help, we can overcome the evil one. There is more on this in the sections about Satan and God.

We should submit to God.

God is not oneness, monism, nor in all things, pantheism. There is one God who is separate and above all and we are to humble ourselves before Him.

James 4:7-8

7 Submit yourselves, then, to God. Resist the devil, and he will flee from you. 8 Come near to God and he will come near to you. "NIV"

Seek the truth, and the truth will set you free. Jesus is above all.

He has all power and authority.

Col 2:10

Christ, who is the head over every power and authority. "NIV"

He is over the demons, not only driving them out, but also controlling their speech.

Mark 1:34

34 and Jesus healed many who had various diseases. He also drove out many demons, but he would not let the demons speak because they knew who he was. "NIV"

For further consideration, there were many times when people acknowledged who he was or wanted to shout to the world that he had miraculously healed them. Yet, as with the demons, Jesus admonished them to remain silent because the time had not yet come to reveal who he really was to the world. Therefore, we might conclude that Jesus healed people out of compassion, not for recognition.

Jesus is over all principalities and powers, including the spirit world.

Col 1:16

16 Christ himself is the Creator who made everything in heaven and earth, the things we can see and the things we can't; the spirit world with its kings and kingdoms, its rulers and authorities; all were made by Christ for his own use and glory. "TLB"

In the next section, we will look at what the Bible has to say about Satan. Sadly, he has misled many unwitting souls to follow him on a path to hell.

Section IV

Worshiping Satan

The number of those who acknowledge worshiping Satan is relatively small. However, the majority of people have been led astray by him. Take a close look and contemplate the names and titles the Bible attributes to him.

Satan = the accuser from the Hebrew.

SA'TAN (sa'tan; Heb. satan, Grk. Satanas, an "adversary, opponent"). The chief of fallen spirits.

Scripture Names and Titles. Satan is also called the devil, the dragon, the evil one, the angel of the abyss, the ruler of this world, the prince of the power of the air, the god of this world, Apollyon, Abaddon, Belial, and Beelzebub. But Satan and the devil are the names most frequently given.

(From The New Unger's Bible Dictionary. Originally published by Moody Press of Chicago, Illinois. Copyright (c) 1988.)

What does the Bible say about him?

Originally, Satan was created; full of wisdom, perfect in beauty, and blameless.

> Ezek 28:12-15
>
> 'This is what the Sovereign LORD says:
>
> "'You were the model of perfection, full of wisdom and perfect in beauty. 13 You were in Eden, the garden of God; every precious stone adorned you: ruby, topaz, and emerald, chrysolite, onyx and jasper, sapphire, turquoise, and beryl. Your settings and mountings were made of gold; on the day you were created they were prepared. 14 You were anointed as a guardian cherub, for so I ordained you. You were on the holy mount of God; you walked among the fiery stones. 15 You were blameless in your ways from the day you were created till wickedness was found in you. "NIV"

He was cast out of heaven.

> Ezek 28:16-17
>
> 16 Through your widespread trade you were filled with violence, and you sinned. So I drove you in disgrace from the mount of God, and I expelled you, O guardian cherub, from among the fiery stones. 17 Your heart became proud on account of your beauty, and you corrupted your wisdom because of your splendor. So I threw you to the earth; I made a spectacle of you before kings. NIV

His pride was his downfall; wanting to be like God.

> Isa 14:12-14
>
> 12 How you have fallen from heaven, O morning

star, son of the dawn! You have been cast down to the earth, you who once laid low the nations! 13 You said in your heart, "I will ascend to heaven; I will raise my throne above the stars of God; I will sit enthroned on the mount of assembly, on the utmost heights of the sacred mountain. 14 I will ascend above the tops of the clouds; I will make myself like the Most High." "NIV"

He is able to transform himself into an angel of light.

Notice that even his servants can masquerade as righteous.

2 Cor 11:14-15

Satan himself masquerades as an angel of light. 15 It is not surprising, then, if his servants masquerade as servants of righteousness. "NIV"

He is the ruler of this world.

Eph 2:2

2 in which you used to live when you followed the ways of this world and of the ruler of the kingdom of the air, the spirit who is now at work in those who are disobedient. "NIV"

1 John 5:19

19 the whole world is under the control of the evil one. "NIV"

He is the father of lies.

On a personal note, I must admit that I do not even like having a conversation with a liar. What is the point? I once had a friend who would lie even when the truth sounded better. Obviously, he could not be counted on, nor did I value his opinion.

John 8:44

44 You belong to your father, the devil, and you want to carry out your father's desire. He was a murderer from the beginning, not holding to the truth, for there is no truth in him. When he lies, he speaks his native language, for he is a liar and the father of lies. "NIV"

He has a well-developed scheme to oppose the followers of Jesus.

In this passage, we are admonished to seek God's protection because the devil is a mighty opponent.

Eph 6:11-12

11 Put on the full armor of God so that you can take your stand against the devil's schemes. 12 For our struggle is not against flesh and blood, but against the rulers, against the authorities, against the powers of this dark world and against the spiritual forces of evil in the heavenly realms. "NIV"

He uses deception.

2 Cor 11:3

3 But I am afraid that just as Eve was deceived by the serpent's cunning, your minds may somehow be led astray from your sincere and pure devotion to Christ. "NIV"

He roams the earth seeking whomever he will devour.

1 Peter 5:8

8 Be self-controlled and alert. Your enemy the devil prowls around like a roaring lion looking for someone to devour. "NIV"

He is limited in power so that believers are able to resist him.

James 4:7

7 Submit yourselves, then, to God. Resist the devil, and he will flee from you. "NIV"

What the Bible teaches about demons.

We touched on demons in the last section.

Satan is over demons.

Demons are supernatural beings typically associated with evil. Many believe they are fallen angels. We all have a choice, even angels. We can accept God, and come to Him on his terms, or we may choose to do our own thing. We are not forced to do anything, but our choices do have eternal consequences.

They know God and fear Him.

James 2:19

19 You believe that there is one God. Good! Even the demons believe that-and shudder. "NIV"

Looking at the following example from the Bible, we can learn many things about demons. They can possess people, and when they do, the person can have superior strength, and appear to be out of their mind.

Mark 5:2-13

2 When Jesus got out of the boat, a man with an evil spirit came from the tombs to meet him. 3 This man lived in the tombs, and no one could bind him any more, not even with a chain. 4 For he had often been chained hand and foot, but he tore the chains apart and broke the irons on his feet. No one was strong enough to subdue him. 5 Night and day among the tombs and in the hills he would cry out and cut himself with stones.

They recognize Jesus as the Son of God, with authority and power over them.

6 When he saw Jesus from a distance, he ran and fell on his knees in front of him. 7 He shouted at the top of his voice, "What do you want with me, Jesus, Son of the Most High God? Swear to God that you won't torture me!" 8 For Jesus had said to him, "Come out of this man, you evil spirit!"

9 Then Jesus asked him, "What is your name?"

"My name is Legion," he replied, "for we are many." 10 And he begged Jesus again and again not to send them out of the area.

11 A large herd of pigs was feeding on the nearby hillside. 12 The demons begged Jesus, "Send us among the pigs; allow us to go into them." 13 He gave them permission, and the evil spirits came out and went into the pigs. The herd, about two thousand in number, rushed down the steep bank into the lake and were drowned. "NIV"

Demons work to oppose the plans of God.

There is a spiritual battle going on. In this example from the Bible, we see that even though a messenger was sent from God, the forces of evil were able to detain him.

Dan 10:12-13

12 Then he continued, "Do not be afraid, Daniel.

> *Since the first day that you set your mind to gain understanding and to humble yourself before your God, your words were heard, and I have come in response to them. 13 But the prince of the Persian kingdom resisted me twenty-one days. Then Michael, one of the chief princes, came to help me, because I was detained there with the king of Persia. "NIV"*

God is above all, including Satan and the demons.

There are many instances in the Bible where Jesus healed people by driving out demons. In the following passage, we see that Jesus even delegated this power and authority to his apostles.

> *Luke 9:1*
>
> *9:1 When Jesus had called the Twelve together, he gave them power and authority to drive out all demons "NIV"*

They will be judged.

> *2 Peter 2:4-5*
>
> *4 For if God did not spare angels when they sinned, but sent them to hell, putting them into gloomy dungeons to be held for judgment; "NIV"*

Satan and his followers are doomed.

> *Matt 25:41*
>
> *41 "Then he will say to those on his left, 'Depart from me, you who are cursed, into the eternal fire prepared for the devil and his angels. "NIV"*

God has decreed and written about their final outcome.

The final destination for Satan and his followers is the lake of fire where they are in endless torment.

> *Rev 20:10*
>
> *10 And the devil, who deceived them, was thrown into the lake of burning sulfur, where the beast and the false prophet had been thrown. They will be tormented day and night forever and ever. "NIV"*

Many unwittingly follow Satan.

The Bible says, "No one can serve two masters." While this passage actually refers to God and money, it illustrates we cannot serve both God and Satan.

Dear friends, do not be deceived.

In an earlier passage, we saw that even Satan's servants masquerade as servants of righteousness. It is no wonder then that we are warned about being misled.

> *1 John 4:1-2*
>
> *4:1 Dear friends, do not believe every spirit, but test the spirits to see whether they are from God, because many false prophets have gone out into the world. 2 This is how you can recognize the Spirit of God: Every spirit that acknowledges that Jesus Christ has come in the flesh is from God, "NIV"*

As the pie chart, "Where are you in relationship to God?" illustrates, Satan misleads most people.

> *Matt 7:13*
>
> *For wide is the gate and broad is the road that leads*

to destruction, and many enter through it. "NIV"

The purpose of this book is to help you understand the choices before you. My goal is enabling you to make an informed decision about things that have eternal consequences.

Section V

Atheists, deny that God exists

Some hardliners deny God, but they cannot prove He does not exist. Actually, that is impossible. Many thinking of themselves in this category probably doubt, rather than deny, the existence of God. The "don't know, don't care" group is covered in the next section. Here we will only touch on a couple of issues: creation versus evolution, and is the Bible believable?

What about "Evolution vs. Creation?"

This seems to be a battle between a logical scientific theory, and an unscientific illogical account of creation as recorded in the Bible. There continue to be many books written on the subject, and I defer to them for your more in-depth study. Recently, the concept of *intelligent design* has been put forth in opposition to that of *random chance*.

For those who believe the theory of evolution has been proven by science, it has not. In fact, it is just the opposite.

What are the odds?

What are the odds that life, in its simplest forms, could originate on earth by chance?

Quoting from *Creation vs. Evolution, What You Need To Know,* John Anderberg & John Weldon, 1998, "This is a physical and mathematical impossibility. This idea violates the law of biogenesis. That life originates only from life, as well as other scientific laws, is proven false by the science of probability. The chance that life could evolve from non-life is statistically zero no matter how old the universe. Many evolutionists have conceded that if the odds of evolution occurring are just 1 in 10 to the 250th power. (The figure 1 with 250 zeros)

Impossible. Borel's single law of chance tells us that when the chance exceeds 1 chance in 10 to the 50th power, absolutely no chance remains for an event to occur. Even evolutionary scientists have estimated the chance that life could evolve at 1 in 10 to the 100,000,000,000 power.

The eye is truly incredible.

Did you know that the eye has 40,000,000 nerve endings, the focusing muscles move an estimated 100,000 times a day, and the retina contains 137,000,000 light sensitive cells?

Even Charles Darwin said,

> "To suppose that the eye could have been formed by natural selection seems I freely confess, absurd in the highest degree."

How could anyone in his right mind think that eyes formed by mere chance? Yet, the eye is only a small part of the most sophisticated part of creation, the human body.

George Gallup, the famous statistician, said,

> "I could prove God statistically; take the human body alone; the chance that all the functions of the individual would just happen, is a statistical monstrosity."

Albert Einstein said,

> *"Everyone who is seriously interested in the pursuit of science becomes convinced that a spirit is manifest in the laws of the universe—a spirit vastly superior to man, and one in the face of which our modest powers must feel humble."*

Because of the "creation," no one has an excuse.

According to the Bible, we should all recognize that there is a God just by observing the world we live in.

> Rom 1:20
>
> 20 For since the creation of the world God's invisible qualities-his eternal power and divine nature-have been clearly seen, being understood from what has been made, so that men are without excuse. "NIV"

What about science and the Bible?

The following is from the book *Scientific Facts in the Bible* that was available on the website at livingwaters.com at the time of this writing.

> *The Bible and Earth's Free-float in Space*
>
> *At a time when it was believed that the earth sat on a large animal or a giant (1500 B.C.), the Bible spoke of the earth's free float in space: "He . . . hangs the earth upon nothing" (Job 26:7). Science didn't discover that the earth hangs upon nothing until 1650.*
>
> *The Scriptures Speak of an Invisible Structure*
>
> *Only in recent years has science discovered that everything we see is composed of things that we cannot*

see—invisible atoms. In Hebrews 11:3, written 2,000 years ago, Scripture tells us that the "things which are seen were not made of things which do appear."

The Bible Reveals that the Earth is Round

The Scriptures tell us that the earth is round: "It is he that sits upon the circle of the earth" (Isaiah 40:22). The word translated "circle" here is the Hebrew word chuwg, which is also translated "circuit" or "compass" (depending on the context). That is, it indicates something spherical, rounded, or arched — not something that is flat or square. The book of Isaiah was written sometime between 740 and 680 B.C. This is at least 300 years before Aristotle suggested, in his book On the Heavens, that the earth might be a sphere. It was another 2,000 years later (at a time when science believed that the earth was flat) that the Scriptures inspired Christopher Columbus to sail around the world.

The Bible and the Science of Oceanography

Matthew Maury (1806–1873) is considered the father of oceanography. He noticed the expression "paths of the sea" in Psalm 8:8 (written 2,800 years ago) and said, "If God said there are paths in the sea, I am going to find them." Maury then took God at His word and went looking for these paths, and we are indebted to his discovery of the warm and cold continental currents. His book on oceanography remains a basic text on the subject and is still used in universities.

The Bible and Radio Waves

God asked Job a very strange question in 1500 B.C. He asked, "Can you send lightnings, that they may *go, and say to you, Here we are?" (Job 38:35). This appears to be a scientifically ludicrous statement — that light can be sent, and then manifest itself in speech. But did you know that all electromagnetic radiation —from radio waves to x-rays—travels at the speed of light? This is why you can have instantaneous wireless communication with someone on the other side of the earth. The fact that light could be sent and then manifest itself in speech wasn't discovered by science until 1864 (3,300 years later), when "British scientist James Clerk Maxwell suggested that electricity and light waves were two forms of the same thing" (Modern Century Illustrated Encyclopedia).*

The Bible and Entropy

Three different places in the Bible (Isaiah 51:6; Psalm 102:25,26; and Hebrews 1:11) indicate that the earth is wearing out. This is what the Second Law of Thermodynamics (the Law of Increasing Entropy) states: that in all physical processes, every ordered system over time tends to become more disordered. Everything is running down and wearing out as energy is becoming less and less available for use. That means the universe will eventually "wear out" to the extent that (theoretically speaking) there will be a "heat death" and therefore no more energy available for use. This wasn't discovered by science until recently, but the Bible states it in concise terms.

The Bible and the Water Cycle

The Scriptures inform us, "All the rivers run into the sea; yet the sea is not full; unto the place from whence the rivers come, there they return again" (Ecclesiastes 1:7). This statement alone may not seem profound.

But, when considered with other biblical passages, it becomes all the more remarkable. For example, the Mississippi River dumps approximately 518 billion gallons of water every 24 hours into the Gulf of Mexico. Where does all that water go? And that's just one of thousands of rivers. The answer lies in the hydrologic cycle, so well brought out in the Bible.

Ecclesiastes 11:3 states that "if the clouds be full of rain, they empty themselves upon the earth." Look at the Bible's concise words in Amos 9:6: "He ... calls for the waters of the sea, and pours them out upon the face of the earth." The idea of a complete water cycle was not fully understood by science until the seventeenth century. However, more than two thousand years prior to the discoveries of Pierre Perrault, Edme Mariotte, Edmund Halley, and others, the Scriptures clearly spoke of a water cycle.

The Bible and the First Law of Thermodynamics

The Scriptures say, "Thus the heavens and the earth were finished, and all the host of them" (Genesis 2:1). The original Hebrew uses the past definite tense for the verb "finished," indicating an action completed in the past, never again to occur. The creation was "finished" — once and for all. That is exactly what the First Law of Thermodynamics says. This law (often referred to as the Law of the Conservation of Energy and/or Mass) states that neither matter nor energy can be either created or destroyed.

It was because of this Law that Sir Fred Hoyle's "Steady-State" (or "Continuous Creation") Theory was discarded. Hoyle stated that at points in the universe called "irtrons," matter (or energy) was constantly being created. But, the First Law states just the opposite. Indeed, there is no "creation" ongoing today. It is "finished" exactly as the Bible states.

The Bible and Ship Dimensions

In Genesis 6, God gave Noah the dimensions of the 1.5 million cubic foot ark he was to build. In 1609 at Hoorn in Holland, a ship was built after that same pattern (30:5:3), revolutionizing shipbuilding. By 1900 every large ship on the high seas was inclined toward the proportions of the ark (verified by "Lloyd's Register of Shipping" in the World Almanac).

The Bible and Meteorological Laws

The Scriptures describe a "cycle" of air currents two thousand years before scientists discovered them: "The wind goes toward the south, and turns about unto the north; it whirls about continually, and the wind returns again according to his circuits" (Ecclesiastes 1:6). We now know that air around the earth turns in huge circles, clockwise in one hemisphere and counter-clockwise in the other.

The Bible and Science

"In antiquity and in what is called the Dark Ages, men did not know what they now know about humanity and the cosmos. They did not know the lock but they possessed they key, which is God. Now many have excellent descriptions of the lock, but they have lost the key. The proper solution is union between religion and science. We should be owners of the lock and the key. The fact is that as science advances, it discovers what was said thousands of years ago in the Bible." Richard Wurmbrand, Proofs of God's Existence

Further Contents of this book:

Chapter 2 - The Incredible Book of Job

Chapter 3 - Medical Science and the Bible

Chapter 4 - Science and Genesis

Chapter 5 - Scientists and the Bible

Chapter 6 - Biology and the Bible

Chapter 7 - The Bible's 100% Accurate Prophecies

Chapter 8 - Astronomy and the Bible

Chapter 9 - Historical Figures and the Bible

Chapter 10 - Archaeology and the Bible

Chapter 11 - The Bible's Historical Accuracy

Chapter 12 - Evolution and the Bible

Chapter 13 - Science and Evolution

There is much more evidence to prove we can trust the Bible and that God exists than speculation that He does not.

The science of probability proves we can trust the Bible.

As we saw earlier in the section on Monotheism, there were forty-eight prophecies fulfilled in one person, Jesus. The odds of even eight prophecies fulfilled in Jesus in the last week of his life are one in one hundred million billion. And, since several different people, living on different continents, from different cultures, made these prophecies over a period of hundreds of years, it both proves that Jesus is the Christ, and that the Bible is equally reliable.

What if it matters to God what you believe?

If you are living your life like there is no God, you had better be right.

If God does not exist, your expectations probably go something like this. Once you are born, you live your life with one or two philosophies: "Leave the earth a better place than you found it," or "Whoever dies with the most toys, fame, fortune or power, wins." When you die, you simply cease to exist. Your whole life is summed up in what you accomplished in life, and what you leave behind.

On the other hand, if God exists, you may spend eternity regretting your mistake.

As the passages in the last section illustrate, Jesus has command over the spirit world. We saw that even the demons believe in one God and tremble in fear. Obviously, they know something that we should heed.

> *Heb 10:31*
>
> *31 It is a dreadful thing to fall into the hands of the living God. "NIV"*
>
> *Ps 111:10*
>
> *10 The fear of the LORD is the beginning of wisdom; "NIV"*

According to the Bible, God will judge us all.

> *Rom 14:10-12*
>
> *For we will all stand before God's judgment seat. 11 It is written:*
>
> *"'As surely as I live,' says the Lord, 'every knee will bow before me;*

every tongue will confess to God.'"

12 So then, each of us will give an account of himself to God. "NIV"

Therefore, if you think it would be wise to find out on what basis God judges us? You can find the answer scattered throughout this book and summarized in the section about God.

Section VI

Agnostics, do not know or do not care if God exists

At one time in my life, I could have fit into this category. I had not read the Bible yet and I was confused by what I had been taught in school about evolution.

Some might say they have not given much thought about God. Others may be overwhelmed with the magnitude of the many beliefs and have just given up trying to decide between them. Many stay away from the subject. You have probably heard that to avoid arguments do not discuss religion or politics.

Actually, I like discussing anything, as long as we can share our thoughts in a respectful way. I do not like arguments or debates. By my definition, a debate is a controlled argument. In a discussion, you exchange ideas, seeking the truth. In the end, you may change your opinion, or just agree to disagree. In any event, you have shown respect by listening, and evaluating what is said.

My purpose in writing this book is to present information so that you can make an informed decision about God. To help you know that God exists, where you are in correlation to Him, and the relationship He wants with you. Later in this book, you will be prompted to make a choice, and my hope for you is that you are ready.

In this section, I have included a look at a couple of religious beliefs. In relating to them, we can see that we cannot only know about God, but we can have a relationship with Him.

However, my concern is for those who are apathetic. They just do not seem to care one way or another about God. This lackadaisical approach to God is dreadful and carries dire consequences. The Bible tells us that no one has an excuse. Because of the creation, anyone who has ever lived should recognize there is a God. Therefore, I implore you to carefully consider everything presented here.

Do not wait until it is too late.

I once attended the funeral of the wife of a friend of mine. I did not really know her; I had only been introduced once. My attendance was not out of grief; I was just there to support my friend.

She was not old, probably in her mid-thirties. Her death was anticipated because she had been battling cancer for some time. The service was held in a small chapel on the grounds of the cemetery. It was a rainy day and the place was filled with friends and family. She had not known the person conducting the service. He was just a local clergyman who was on call by the funeral home to perform funerals when the person who dies does not have anyone else. He began with, "She didn't know if God exists, but she hoped He does." At which point I did feel sad for her.

Like others, she thought that she probably lived a life that would be acceptable to God. Comparing herself to other people, she felt good about herself. She was a faithful wife and mother. She worked outside the home, but still found time to help her kids with schoolwork. She did not attend a church but she gave to charities and lived by the adage of treating others the way you would like to be treated.

Anyway, she might say, "If there is a God, isn't he a God of Love? I cannot believe he would send anybody to hell. Moreover, even if he did, I have been good. I don't think that going to church counts, it's how you live your life."

She, like most people will say they are good enough when they compare themselves to others. However, what if God's standard is comparing us to Him? What if He is so holy that he cannot permit anything less than pure to come into his presence? Anything dirty, defiled, sinful, must be cleansed or it is not allowed. As with Gold, the impurities must be removed to get to a pure state. As with God, we must be sanctified to enter into His presence in heaven.

In that case, instead of wondering why God would send you to hell, you might ask yourself, "Why should He let me into heaven?" If your answer has been, "I've been good," His answer just might be, "By whose standards?"

If you are thinking that it seems impossible to live up to God's standards, that nobody is perfect, then you are on the right track. If it were up to us, it would be hopeless. However, nothing is impossible for God. The good news is, God can do for us that we cannot do for ourselves. There is more on this contained elsewhere in this book, and especially in the section about God.

Next, we will explore two belief systems that have many adherents. One has concluded that the goal of life is to escape suffering and enter into an unknown realm where consciousness ceases to exist. The other has some foggy notion of eternal bliss. Their concept of God has been minimized to the point of transforming God into a concept called heaven.

Buddhism

Introduction

Siddhartha Gautama founded Buddhism about the 6th century B.C. He was born into an area where Hinduism was dominant and he was greatly influenced by it. As the caste system goes, he was born into one of the upper castes, the warriors. According to tradition, his father was very protective. He kept Siddhartha from witnessing any form of suffering. However, one day, Siddhartha ventured from home and really saw misery for the first time. This had a profound effect on him and changed his life forever.

He left his wife and family at home and went on a quest to end pain, grief, and unhappiness. For about six years, he wandered in search of answers. He was obviously very compassionate and wanted to help people. He was disillusioned with wealth and prominence, observing that neither could relieve misery, and could actually cause suffering for others. Finally, in despair, he concluded it was impossible for him to find a way to cure the ills of mankind. Influenced by his Hindu background, he found formulated a solution to this dilemma.

Let us follow the thought process as he may have gone through it. He was taught to believe in *karma;* the law of cause and effect, and reincarnation. However, these were disproved as we saw in the section on Hinduism. Nevertheless, he deviated from the belief in many Gods into the concept of nirvana and that God is a void. This might have happened because he was sensitive to the suffering of people. He might have wondered, as many do, if there were a God, why would He allow people to suffer? Therefore, he reasoned that God must be aloof and unknowable; otherwise, He would have compassion on mankind. Hence, God is a void!

Conclusion: Life is suffering. You escape the cycle of reincarnation by progressing in your goodness and knowledge to become one with an unknowable God, or void.

The finale of this process has been called *enlightenment.* Siddhartha Gautama became the *Buddha,* or "enlightened one." The Buddha did not have special insight; he had compassion. His answer to dealing with pain, suffering and hardship was to avoid reality. He concluded that since life is an illusion, we could endure anything,

Basic beliefs

The Buddha was sensitive to the plight of others. He was looking for an end to pain and suffering. He wondered why a loving God would allow harm to come to those He had created. Since he could not find an answer, he gave up on God. He concluded that God is an abstract and therefore unknowable. Life is a series of miseries, and the ultimate goal is to escape the cycle of reincarnation

There are "Four Noble Truths."

▶ First: Life consists of suffering

▶ Second: Everything is impermanent and ever changing

▶ Third: The way to liberate oneself from suffering is by eliminating all desire

▶ Fourth: Following the "Eight-Fold Path" can eliminate desire

These eight points can be categorized according to three major sections.

▶ Wisdom

→Right Understanding

→Right Thought

▶ Ethical Conduct

→Right Speech

→Right Action

→Right Livelihood

▶ Mental Discipline

→Right Effort

→Right Awareness

→Right Meditation

The first two points serve as a foundation. For example, when one has "right understanding," he or she sees the universe as an illusion. Therefore, the "I" does not exist; there is no self. When "right thought" follows it means to renounce all attachment to the desires and thoughts of self.

Does it matter how we live our life?

Hinduism influenced the Buddha, so it comes as no surprise that some of their teachings are incorporated into Buddhism, such as karma and reincarnation. With this philosophy, it does not matter as much how you live your life because you always get another chance. You just keep coming back until you have worked off all your bad karma.

What are they striving for?

Since the Buddha believed that life is suffering, the ultimate goal is escaping the cycle by attaining nirvana.

What happens when we die?

We are reincarnated until we become enlightened and attain nirvana. At which point, all desire and individual consciousness is extinguished.

What is the appeal?

It promotes self-improvement and a path toward inner peace.

What are some apparent problems with this set of beliefs?

As we have seen, the Bible demonstrates that there is no reincarnation. We looked closely at that and karma in the section on Hinduism. Since Hinduism influenced the Buddha, and Hinduism itself is a philosophical belief system of unknown origin, we have to question the philosophical teachings of the Buddha. After all, he just added to a questionable belief system.

Furthermore, it renders God irrelevant. It is too bad that Siddhartha Gautama did not go looking for God when he was on his quest to become enlightened.

What does the Bible tell us?

God cares about us and wants a relationship with us.

That is why He sent His Son. The shortest verse in the Bible is "Jesus wept."

We can learn much from this. The circumstances were when Lazarus, the brother of Mary and Martha, had died. These three were close friends of Jesus. Yet, although Jesus had healed many, when he heard that Lazarus was ill, he remained at a distance for a few more days. He even knew Lazarus was dying, but to his grief, and God's glory, he did not intervene. The purpose in all of this was to teach us about the resurrection.

After the allotted time, Jesus went to Lazarus to bring him back from the dead. As he approached, Martha met him.

> *John 11:21-27*
>
> *21 "Lord," Martha said to Jesus, "if you had been here, my brother would not have died. 22 But I know that even now God will give you whatever you ask."*
>
> *23 Jesus said to her, "Your brother will rise again." 24 Martha answered, "I know he will rise again in the resurrection at the last day."*
>
> *Her faith was great. She had already witnessed many miracles performed by Jesus, and now he was going to validate her faith in the resurrection.*
>
> *25 Jesus said to her, "I am the resurrection and the life. He who believes in me will live, even though he dies; 26 and whoever lives and believes in me will never die. Do you believe this?"*
>
> *27 "Yes, Lord," she told him, "I believe that you are the Christ, the Son of God, who was to come into the world." "NIV"*

Her sister Mary also expressed a similar faith

John 11:32-35

32 When Mary reached the place where Jesus was and saw him, she fell at his feet and said, "Lord, if you had been here, my brother would not have died."

In his humanity, Jesus can relate to our sorrows, even to the loss of a loved one.

33 When Jesus saw her weeping, and the Jews who had come along with her also weeping, he was deeply moved in spirit and troubled. 34 "Where have you laid him?" he asked. "Come and see, Lord," they replied.

35 Jesus wept. "NIV"

Through Jesus, we can relate to God, and He to us.

Although Jesus was about to restore life to Lazarus, he wept. He had compassion and felt the sorrow of someone losing a loved one. He felt Mary and Martha's pain. This demonstrates how Jesus can relate to us, and how we might feel. It should also be a reminder that when we stand before the judgment seat of God, that we are without any excuses. None of us will be able to offer a plea like, "But God, you don't know what it was like for me," because He does. Continuing:

John 11:36-45

36 Then the Jews said, "See how he loved him!" 37 But some of them said, "Could not he who opened the eyes of the blind man have kept this man from dying?"

Notice that even the scoffers acknowledged the miraculous healings that were done by Jesus. However, what he did next was done in such a way as foretelling his own death, burial, and resurrection.

38 Jesus, once more deeply moved, came to the tomb. It was a cave with a stone laid across the entrance. 39 "Take away the stone," he said.

"But, Lord," said Martha, the sister of the dead man, "by this time there is a bad odor, for he has been there four days." 40 Then Jesus said, "Did I not tell you that if you believed, you would see the glory of God?" 41 So they took away the stone. Then Jesus looked up and said, "Father, I thank you that you have heard me. 42 I knew that you always hear me, but I said this for the benefit of the people standing here, that they may believe that you sent me."

43 When he had said this, Jesus called in a loud voice, "Lazarus, come out!" 44 The dead man came out, his hands and feet wrapped with strips of linen, and a cloth around his face.

Jesus said to them, "Take off the grave clothes and let him go."

45 Therefore many of the Jews who had come to visit Mary, and had seen what Jesus did, put their faith in him. "NIV"

The next passage tells us that while some revered Jesus as the Son of God, others wanted to kill him and destroy his following. They were more concerned with their own power and authority as religious leaders than they were about God.

John 12:9-11

9 Meanwhile a large crowd of Jews found out that Jesus was there and came, not only because of him but also to see Lazarus, whom he had raised from the dead. 10 So the chief priests made plans to kill Lazarus

> as well, 11 for on account of him many of the Jews were going over to Jesus and putting their faith in him. "NIV"

They wanted to remove any evidence, destroying the miracle, Lazarus and the miracle worker, Jesus. In the next section, we will see who is really behind the opposition to Jesus.

God's purpose in all of this was to teach us about the resurrection. Many of the people who witnessed Jesus raise Lazarus from the dead were also witnesses to the resurrection of Jesus. Furthermore, as we saw earlier, when Jesus was raised from the dead, many others were too, thereby giving us further eyewitness testimony proving the resurrection.

> *Matt 27:52-53*
>
> 52 The tombs broke open and the bodies of many holy people who had died were raised to life. 53 They came out of the tombs, and after Jesus' resurrection, they went into the holy city and appeared to many people. "NIV"

He has compassion for us.

As we shall discuss later, Jesus laid down his own life it was not taken from him. He had compassion for us and took our place, submitting to a horrible, painful death to pay the price for our sins. This was done as only Jesus could do, to reconcile us with a Holy God who loves us, but who is also just and must punish sin.

> *Rom 6:23*
>
> 23 For the wages of sin is death, but the gift of God is eternal life in Christ Jesus our Lord. "NIV"

In another instance, Jesus taught about how God sees us and cares for us.

Matt 5:1-12

5:1 Now when he saw the crowds, he went up on a mountainside and sat down. His disciples came to him, 2 and he began to teach them, saying:

3 "Blessed are the poor in spirit, for theirs is the kingdom of heaven.

4 Blessed are those who mourn, for they will be comforted.

5 Blessed are the meek, for they will inherit the earth.

6 Blessed are those who hunger and thirst for righteousness, for they will be filled.

7 Blessed are the merciful, for they will be shown mercy.

8 Blessed are the pure in heart, for they will see God.

9 Blessed are the peacemakers, for they will be called sons of God.

10 Blessed are those who are persecuted because of righteousness, for theirs is the kingdom of heaven.

11 "Blessed are you when people insult you, persecute you and falsely say all kinds of evil against you because of me.

12 Rejoice and be glad, because great is your reward in heaven, for in the same way they persecuted the prophets who were before you. "NIV"

We can also get a glimpse from this passage of what God would like us to be like.

The loving kindness demonstrated by Jesus.

He healed the blind, lame, and even raised the dead. A number of times he also cast out demons, demonstrating that he is over the spirit world. In one of the following passages, Jesus even told the evil spirits to keep silent. They were declaring Jesus the Son of God, but it was not the right time or place.

Matt 8:16-17

16 When evening came, many who were demon-possessed were brought to him, and he drove out the spirits with a word and healed all the sick. 17 This was to fulfill what was spoken through the prophet Isaiah:

"He took up our infirmities

and carried our diseases." "NIV"

He did it out of his compassion for us, not for his glory. Sometimes he would heal people and then tell them to keep silent about it.

Matt 12:14-18

14 But the Pharisees went out and plotted how they might kill Jesus.

15 Aware of this, Jesus withdrew from that place. Many followed him, and he healed all their sick, 16 warning them not to tell who he was. 17 This was to fulfill what was spoken through the prophet Isaiah:

18 "Here is my servant whom I have chosen,

the one I love, in whom I delight;

I will put my Spirit on him, "NIV"

Matt 14:14

14 When Jesus landed and saw a large crowd, he had compassion on them and healed their sick. "NIV"

Mark 1:32-34

32 That evening after sunset the people brought to Jesus all the sick and demon possessed. 33 The whole town gathered at the door, 34 and Jesus healed many who had various diseases. "NIV"

Mark 10:51-52

51 "What do you want me to do for you?" Jesus asked him.

The blind man said, "Rabbi, I want to see."

52 "Go," said Jesus, "your faith has healed you." Immediately he received his sight and followed Jesus along the road. "NIV"

Luke 4:40

40 When the sun was setting, the people brought to Jesus all who had various kinds of sickness, and laying his hands on each one, he healed them. "NIV"

Luke 8:50-56

50 Hearing this, Jesus said to Jairus, "Don't be afraid; just believe, and she will be healed."

51 When he arrived at the house of Jairus, he did not let anyone go in with him except Peter, John and James, and the child's father and mother. 52 Meanwhile, all the people were wailing and mourning for her. "Stop wailing," Jesus said. "She is not dead but asleep."

> *53 They laughed at him, knowing that she was dead. 54 But he took her by the hand and said, "My child, get up!" 55 Her spirit returned, and at once she stood up. Then Jesus told them to give her something to eat. 56 Her parents were astonished, but he ordered them not to tell anyone what had happened. "NIV"*

> *Luke 9:42-43*

> *42 Even while the boy was coming, the demon threw him to the ground in a convulsion. But Jesus rebuked the evil spirit, healed the boy, and gave him back to his father. 43 And they were all amazed at the greatness of God. "NIV"*

> *John 5:13*

> *13 The man who was healed had no idea who it was, for Jesus had slipped away into the crowd that was there. "NIV"*

There were many instances recorded in the Bible when Jesus would heal someone and either just slip away unnoticed or admonish the person, he had just healed to tell no one. As he did this, he was demonstrating that he had no other motive than his compassion for us.

There are more promises to comfort us contained in scripture. As you read these, picture the kind of relationship God wants with us.

> *Heb 13:5-6*

> *because God has said, "Never will I leave you; never will I forsake you."*

> *6 So we say with confidence, "The Lord is my helper; I will not be afraid.*

What can man do to me?" "NIV"

Isa 40:28-29

The LORD is the everlasting God, the Creator of the ends of the earth. He will not grow tired or weary, and his understanding no one can fathom. 29 He gives strength to the weary and increases the power of the weak. "NIV"

Ps 55:22

22 Cast your cares on the LORD

and he will sustain you;

he will never let the righteous fall. "NIV"

1 Peter 5:6-7

6 Humble yourselves, therefore, under God's mighty hand, that he may lift you up in due time. 7 Cast all your anxiety on him because he cares for you. "NIV"

John 8:12

12 When Jesus spoke again to the people, he said, "I am the light of the world. Whoever follows me will never walk in darkness, but will have the light of life." "NIV"

Ps 27:1

The LORD is my light and my salvation--

whom shall I fear?

The LORD is the stronghold of my life--

of whom shall I be afraid? "NIV"

Matt 11:28

28 "Come to me, all you who are weary and burdened, and I will give you rest. "NIV"

Deut 33:27

27 The eternal God is your refuge "NIV"

There is good news for all of us. We can know God. He has revealed Himself throughout the Bible. God wants us to understand that although He is God of All, He wants a relationship with us as individuals. The aforementioned passages are just as relevant today as when they were written.

Next, and in the section about God, we will see that our relationship with Him can be as Father to child.

Confucianism

Introduction

Confucianism is better described as a philosophy-based belief system than a religion. It is a set of values and moral codes, with emphasis on a strong work ethic and family.

The founder was the Duke of Chou 551-497 B.C. *Confucius* is the Latinized version of the Chinese name K'ung Fu-tzu or Grand Master K'ung.

His quest began during a time of great turmoil between different factions in a region along the Yellow River in China. There had been a movement to unite people through ritualistic music. Yet, by the time of Confucius, it was evident it was not working. However, he was committed to the cause, hoping to bring peace and security to the region.

Predominately an eastern belief system, the adherents include Chinese, Japanese, Korean, and Vietnamese. In round numbers, an estimate of those influenced by Confucianism is estimated at about 1.5 billion people.

Basic beliefs

It is primarily an ethical system. God does not seem personal, or even relevant. If anything, God has been redefined as a concept called heaven.

Confucius occasionally made statements about the existence of otherworldly beings that sounded distinctly agnostic and humanistic.

Does it matter how we live our life?

It is oriented toward living one's life so that it will have an eternal influence on the ethical thoughts and values of their descendants. Highly respected are giving words of wisdom, doing good works, and being loyal and trustworthy.

What are they striving for?

They believe each there is an ideal goodness residing in each of us. The goal then is for us to actualize our good nature, thereby realizing an ideal state of life, living up to our full potential.

Confucius' concept of humaneness is probably best expressed in the Confucian version of the Golden Rule phrased in the negative: "Do not do to others what you would not like them to do to you."

What happens when we die?

If we live according to the principles of Confucianism, we will leave a moral and ethical legacy.

Attaining heaven is not a concern. Heaven is sometimes perceived as personal, but at other times, it is simply a creative moral power and an impersonal principle.

What is the appeal?

It is nice to think that within us is ideal goodness. Confucianism encourages us to get in touch with it and let it come out. By working hard, living to the best of our ability, respecting our elders, rulers, we can leave an ethical and moral legacy.

What are some apparent problems with this set of beliefs?

By ignoring God, you eliminate the chances for a relationship with Him, here and hereafter.

What does the Bible tell us?

God is not just an abstract concept like heaven. He has revealed Himself in various ways so that we might understand Him, and the relationship He wants with us.

> Heb 1:1-3
>
> *1:1 In the past God spoke to our forefathers through the prophets at many times and in various ways, 2 but in these last days he has spoken to us by his Son, whom he appointed heir of all things, and through whom he made the universe. 3 The Son is the radiance of God's glory and the exact representation of his being, sustaining all things by his powerful word. "NIV"*

He is the creator of everything and everyone. Therefore, he is also over all and deserves our worship as well as our submission to His will. Yet, the Bible says He created us in His own image. That does not mean that He was once a man like us, but that he gave us emotions, and the ability to know right from wrong.

For example, God has emotions like love, hate, anger, grief, and joy. He, who is holy and pure, hates what is impure and unholy like sin. Therefore, it grieves Him when we sin, because it causes division between a holy God and us.

The Bible also says He is jealous. He loves us and wants a relationship with us, but He gets angry and rejects us if we deny Him. Our rejection of God takes many forms. Obviously, to deny His existence, as atheists do, is one way. However, there are more subtle ways. God holds it against us if we seek after other gods, as do Hindus. As we saw in the section on Christian Scientists, God is unique. He declared, "I AM God." And in the section on Mormonism, we saw that, "There is no other God, nor shall there ever be." Beyond that, God considers it spiritual adultery when we place anything ahead of Him in our lives, like fame, fortune, power, etc. However, if we put Him first, and seek His righteousness, He promises to care and provide for us.

Matt 6:33

33 But seek first his kingdom and his righteousness, and all these things will be given to you as well. "NIV"

Throughout the Bible, the message from God is that He wants you to know Him, and that He wants a relationship with you. Rather than being distracted by the things of this world, we are to seek a relationship with Him first.

Our relationship with God can be as a child to a father.

However, notice that this does not mean everyone. It is conditional on our faith.

Gal 3:26

26 You are all sons of God through faith in Christ Jesus, "NIV"

The Bible portrays Him as our Father. If we think in human terms, whether we have had a good relationship with our fathers or not, we do have a perception of what one should be.

Rom 8:15-16

you received the Spirit of sonship. And by him we cry, "Abba, Father." 16 The Spirit himself testifies with our spirit that we are God's children. "NIV"

In the previous passage, "Abba, Father" could be translated as though an infant were calling their father "Daddy."

A loving father would care for us when we were unable to care for ourselves. As infants, he would provide for all our needs. As we learned to walk, he would be near us offering us his hand to steady us. Then he would let us take a few steps on our own. Always near, always caring, but ever giving us a little more freedom. He would allow us to fall in order for us to learn to walk on our own.

Then, at an early age, we typically began our rebellion. They call it the "terrible twos." By that tender age, we have learned what the word "no" means, and we use it often to defy our father. Young as we were our father would try to guide us more than teach us. At that age, we needed food and sleep and could not get everything we wanted just by crying. His love for us was so much that he did what was good for us even though we did not know it at the time.

Then at age three, we really began to communicate, and it seemed that we had an insatiable thirst for knowledge. No matter what our father said to us, our standard response was "Why?" Looking deeper, sometimes it might have been an act of rebellion. Early on, we were beginning to question our fathers' authority. He would welcome our questions and always be eager to teach us. He would overlook our acts of defiance due to our young age.

As we matured, he would balance protecting us with allowing us to make mistakes. He would hope we would heed his warnings about not touching a hot stove, because he knew that he would not always be around to prevent us from being burned. He would be looking ahead to the time when we would be making decisions on our own.

He would take great pleasure as we grew beyond just being guided and started learning. He may help us with our schoolwork or the lessons of life so that we may learn and progress. He would hope that we would listen to him because, in his love for us, he only has our best interests at heart.

Moving beyond protection and guidance, our loving father would instill moral values and ethics, for example:

- ▶ Honor your father and mother
- ▶ Respect your elders
- ▶ Do not commit adultery
- ▶ Do not steal
- ▶ Do not murder
- ▶ Be honest and trustworthy
- ▶ Be diligent in your work
- ▶ Be thankful for what you have
- ▶ Help those in need

If we follow the progression, he would care for us until we were able to care for ourselves. He would warn us because he would not want to see us get hurt. He would instruct us so that we may get along with others, because he would not want his other children to be hurt either. Beyond that, he would hope that we would learn to love others as he does. Then we would teach the young, assist the elderly, and help others in their time of need.

Through all his teachings, our father would be demonstrating his love for us. He would be preparing us for the time when we are on our own. You see the freedom to make choices carries with it the consequences of our poor decisions. At some point, we pass from the age of innocence to the age of accountability.

In the end, we are on our own and free to make choices, including whether to have a relationship with our father or not. He has provided for us, taught us, loves us, and wants an association with us, but now it is up to us to decide what our relationship will be with him. Ultimately our loving father's greatest joy would be for us to return the love he has for us.

▶ Do we return his love?

▶ Do we commune or talk with him?

▶ Do we seek his council?

▶ Do we seek his will, or do we just do our own thing?

▶ Do we desire his company, or do we avoid and hide from Him?

Whatever you feel about your own father, your Father in heaven wants a relationship with you. However, to be of value, it must be mutual, with your desire to have a relationship with Him too. If we allow things to come between us, our relationship suffers. At some point, we might act as though we never even had a father.

As you read the following passages, consider what it means to be adopted by God as your Father in heaven.

> *John 1:12-13*
>
> *12 Yet to all who received him, to those who believed in his name, he gave the right to become children of God- 13 children born not of natural descent, nor of human decision or a husband's will, but born of God. "NIV"*

Jesus taught us how to pray to the Father.

Jesus wants us to understand that our relationship to God is as Father to child.

> *Matt 6:9-14*
>
> *9 "Pray along these lines: 'Our Father in heaven,*

Your relationship with your natural father might seem less than ideal. In this case, we can feel like our relationship with God is as a child with a perfect father. He cares about us, while giving us a certain amount of freedom.

> *we honor your holy name.*

God, who is Holy, deserves all honor, glory, and praise.

> *10 We ask that your kingdom will come now.*

We acknowledge you as LORD of all. We know there is a spiritual battle going on between good and evil and that you will prevail. We anxiously await your kingdom to be established.

> *May your will be done here on earth, just as it is in heaven.*

God, we know that in heaven, everything is done subject to your will. We pray for the time when Satan is defeated, and that you will rule on earth as you do in heaven.

> *11 Give us our food again today, as usual,*

We come before you with our daily needs. While you have been faithful to provide, and sometimes we have abundance, we acknowledge that whatever we have may be gone tomorrow.

12 and forgive us our sins, just as we have forgiven those who have sinned against us.

God, we know that you are just. Sins have consequences. While we acknowledge that we are not required to forgive those who do not ask forgiveness, just as you do not forgive those who do not ask forgiveness from you, we pray that we will freely forgive all those who ask forgiveness. Beyond that, for our own good, we ask you to help us have compassion on those who have not asked for forgiveness. We do not understand their circumstances as you do. For our sake and theirs, God help us to forgive and forget.

13 Don't bring us into temptation but deliver us from the Evil One.

God, we know that you do not tempt us, but you allow temptation. We ask that you give us the wisdom to see sinful situations. Those circumstances which entice us to sin. Please give us the wisdom to avoid them, or the strength to say no when tempted.

We acknowledge that you are a Holy God, and that our sin comes between us and can harm the relationship we can have with you. Please keep us from evil, and the Evil One.

Amen.' "TLB"

A relationship with God, takes more than just acknowledging Him.

Wouldn't we all like a relationship with a loving father, now and forever? This is the message from the Bible. We can know God because He has revealed Himself to us. However, knowing Him is not enough. Revering God in His holiness only reveals our nothingness.

Before we can enter into a relationship with a holy God, we who are unholy must be purified. How this is accomplished is discussed throughout this book, and especially in the section about God. The fact is, we cannot do this on our own, but thank God, He has provided a way to do for us what we cannot do for ourselves.

Section VII

Those seeking to know God

Those in search of God are past wondering if He exists. They believe in a Creator or Supreme Being and want to get a better understanding of Him. What does God expect from us, and what can we anticipate from Him? Is it all about here and now, or is there a hereafter too? What happens when we die?

Let us review and summarize.

The two largest groups, Christians, and Muslims, along with Jews, believe the Bible to be the word of God. The foundations for their beliefs are historical. They trace their roots to a common patriarch, Abraham, by whom God chose to reveal Himself to the world.

Then we have the philosophical religions, chief of which is Hinduism because of the influence it has had on many other religious groups. Its origin is vague. It started as a cultural experience, using dance and rituals as ways of bringing diverse people together. It had little to do with God. As the dances and rituals became more complex, they were written down.

Their spiritual leaders came later. They developed the *caste* system, or food chain, that established the priests at the top, the warriors next, then the merchants, slaves, or underlings, and finally the untouchables. When you look at it, it makes perfect sense for the ones who developed it. The priests put themselves at the top. They established the warriors as second best, which would give them the desire to protect the priests and the caste system as an institution. Next, are the merchants to provide the goods and services we all need. They enjoy a high quality of life and can feel good about themselves while using or abusing others of a lower caste. After all, that is their lot in life. Then there are the slaves, or workers who do the heavy labor, but to keep them in their place, they are told they are at least better than the untouchables. If you can imagine misery, this poor group is below being a slave.

Then, to keep everyone in their place, they introduced the concept of *karma*. A loose definition would be that what goes around comes around. When you do bad things, bad things will repay you. When you do good things, it can work off bad karma.

However, anyone can see that life is not fair. We do not always receive reward and punishment soon after we do something. Therefore, they introduced the concept of reincarnation.

Now here is where the control factor of the caste system really comes in. When your good deeds outweigh your bad and you work off your bad karma, you get to advance to the next level. However, do not even think of moving from one level of the caste to another within your lifetime. That would be counted as bad karma and destine you to be reincarnated into the very level you were trying to move from. That would mean enduring hardship all over again as an untouchable, or whatever, before you would get another opportunity to work of your karma and advance.

Sadly, their ultimate goal is escaping this endless cycle of reincarnation and suffering, by reaching a level where we do not have to come back, finally achieving nirvana.

Buddhism, as with many other religious concepts, draws many beliefs from Hinduism. However, the Buddha had his own ideas about God and nirvana that is even drearier.

With the key concepts of reincarnation and karma, Hinduism has influenced many other belief systems. However, for what should be obvious reasons, they reject the caste system. They place little importance on God, focusing more on living a good life, getting along in this world, and leaving a legacy. Others, drawing from Hinduism, believe life is a learning experience. That through reincarnation, they are on a path of eternal progression. One day, they will have advanced enough that they can break the cycle. They draw on the appeal that one day we will reach a higher place.

No reincarnation, no second chance.

Both karma and reincarnation have been disproved. Like a house of cards, when you remove reincarnation, these belief systems fall apart. Since the early 60's, we have been deluged by Eastern religions or belief systems with philosophical or dubious origins. Some focus on harmony and inner peace above all else. Others have reduced God and/or heaven, to a state of mind. Yet, others seem to show a reverence for the creation when they should be worshiping the creator.

Since the lines are blurred between many of these belief systems, people are confused. To avoid conflict, many just resign themselves to a philosophy of tolerance, concluding that all paths lead to God. Obviously, that is not true. In fact, it is impossible.

Because of the creation, nobody has an excuse for denying God.

Atheists deserve our pity because they are betting their life and future, that there is no God to judge them. However, we have seen that even Charles Darwin questioned the theory of evolution that he put forth.

We can believe the Bible.

According to Judaism, Christianity and Islam, the Bible is the Word of God.

The Bible has been verified through archeological discoveries.

Historical records also validate the truth of Bible.

The Bible proves itself, through the science of probability, by prophecy fulfilled.

The Bible tells us about God.

In the section on Mormons, we saw that there is only one God. He is above all and no matter how good we are or how hard we try; we will never be like Him.

God wants us to know Him.

Because people have been confused as exampled by polytheism, monism, pantheism and paganism, God chose to reveal himself so we can know Him. In the section on Buddhism, we saw Jesus as the Son of God who has compassion on us. In Confucianism, we saw that the Bible teaches we can know God as our Father.

Hell is real.

God loves us and does not want to punish us, but God is just and must punish sin.

In the section about Jehovah's Witnesses, we saw that there is a hell, and it is to be feared. It is endless torment and you do not want yourself or your friends to go there.

> *Luke 12:5*
>
> *5 But I will show you whom you should fear: Fear him who, after the killing of the body, has power to throw you into hell. Yes, I tell you, fear him. "NIV"*

God wants to forgive us so that we can have a relationship with Him.

In Judaism, we saw that God provides a way of forgiveness for our sins.

In Islam, we saw that Jesus alone was born of a virgin, without sin, and was able to forgive sins.

In Catholicism, we discovered that Jesus is our high priest allowing us direct access to God the Father.

Satan wants to deceive us.

Satan is our adversary who leads us away from God. He knows God's standards and is always ready to accuse everyone of falling short thereby denying their entrance into heaven.

What do you anticipate from knowing God?

Health and wealth?

You will be disappointed. While God cares about each of us, it is unrealistic to expect that He will supply everything we want. He might supply our needs, but that is still subject to His will. Let us look at this in overly simplistic terms. What if everyone that believed in God was prosperous and unbelievers were not.? If that were the case, it would not be a question of faith; we would just be motivated by reward and punishment. It is a fact that bad things happen to good people, and vice versa. Therefore, our faith and relationship with God should focus as much on the hereafter as it does on our present situation.

A God you can control?

It is not going to happen. We are subject to God, not the other way around. Therefore, even if you believe in God and pray to Him as though you want your will to be done, it will not have the same effect as if you prayed that His will would be done.

A God who does not judge?

God is merciful, but He is also just. When people humble themselves, and admit wrongdoing, God is willing to forgive. Nevertheless, make no mistake, God is just, and He will punish evildoers. He makes the rules that we are to be judged by, we do not.

A designer God?

There is nothing new under the sun. People have been creating God in their image since the beginning of time. It could be an idol carved of wood or stone, or some image of God, as they want Him to be. A God who agrees with you, allowing everything you like to do, and condemning others who do not meet your standards.

Or, are you truly seeking to understand God?

If you are, that is fantastic! As you will see in the next section, God wants you to know Him and He wants a relationship with you. He knows you better than you know yourself, and He loves you anyway.

You should understand something else. The relationship you

establish with God now will last throughout all eternity.

Good news; God loves people who seek him.

Matt 7:7-8

7 "Ask and it will be given to you; seek and you will find; knock and the door will be opened to you. 8 For everyone who asks receives; he who seeks finds; and to him who knocks, the door will be opened. "NIV"

Are you confused?

Satan is the father of lies and author or confusion.

He is called the god of this age because God is allowing him to tempt and deceive us for now. Nevertheless, the Bible tells us this is all part of God's plan. One day Satan and his followers will be cast into a lake of fire and God's kingdom will be established forever.

2 Cor 4:3-4

3 And even if our gospel is veiled, it is veiled to those who are perishing. 4 The god of this age has blinded the minds of unbelievers, so that they cannot see the light of the gospel of the glory of Christ, who is the image of God. "NIV"

We are warned not to believe everyone.

Matt 7:15

15 "Watch out for false prophets. They come to you in sheep's clothing, but inwardly they are ferocious wolves. "NIV"

God wants us to know the truth.

Throughout the ages, God has revealed Himself and His will for us.

1 Tim 2:3-4

3 This is good, and pleases God our Savior, 4 who wants all men to be saved and to come to a knowledge of the truth. "NIV"

Satan uses many tactics trying to defeat the plan of God.

There is a spiritual battle for our souls, and Satan wins whenever he draws our attention away from God.

He discredits the word of God.

It started in the Garden of Eden. God wanted a relationship with Adam and Eve, undefiled by sin. Since God is Holy, He cannot tolerate any association with sin. Therefore, when Adam and Eve sinned it caused a separation between God and man.

God had told them they could eat anything in the Garden of Eden except one thing. His command carried a warning of dire consequences if they disobeyed.

Gen 2:16-17

16 And the LORD God commanded the man, "You are free to eat from any tree in the garden; 17 but you must not eat from the tree of the knowledge of good and evil, for when you eat of it you will surely die." "NIV"

Before partaking of the fruit, they were incapable of judging right from wrong. Once they knew, there was no excuse. They were now accountable for anything they decided to do, right or wrong, good, or evil.

This is similar to our legal system. A person cannot be held to a contract if they were incapable of understanding it. Likewise, a person cannot be tried for an offense if they are found to be incompetent. What that means is, that they were incapable of understanding the consequence of their actions at the time.

Knowing this, Satan set out to trap Adam and Eve. He knew that through their sin of disobeying God, they would receive the knowledge of good and evil, and therefore suffer the consequences of sin; separation from God. Moreover, through them, all their descendants received the same knowledge.

Satan, appearing as a serpent, got Eve to question God.

Gen 3:1-5

3:1 Now the serpent was more crafty than any of the wild animals the LORD God had made. He said to the woman, "Did God really say, 'You must not eat from any tree in the garden'?"

2 The woman said to the serpent, "We may eat fruit from the trees in the garden, 3 but God did say, 'You must not eat fruit from the tree that is in the middle of the garden, and you must not touch it, or you will die.'"

4 "You will not surely die," the serpent said to the woman. 5 "For God knows that when you eat of it your eyes will be opened, and you will be like God, knowing good and evil." "NIV"

Because of their disobedience, sin entered the entire human race. We have all received the same knowledge and are subject to the same fate.

> *Rom 5:12*
>
> *12 When Adam sinned, sin entered the entire human race. His sin spread death throughout all the world, so everything began to grow old and die, for all sinned. "TLB"*

Good news; there is more to the story.

> *Gen 3:13-15*
>
> *13 Then the LORD God said to the woman, "What is this you have done?"*
>
> *The woman said, "The serpent deceived me, and I ate."*

Therefore, in the beginning, man had been deceived by Satan and turned away from trusting God. As a result, sin entered the world, the consequence of which is death. At first glance, this appears that Satan wins, and God loses. God wanted a relationship with man. Not as Master to slave, nor as a Puppeteer to a puppet, but as Father to child. A relationship has more value when it is not by force but by choice. Nevertheless, sin causes division, which is exactly what Satan wants, our separation from God. However, remember that Satan is a created being.

The Creator is greater than the creation. God is over all.

> *14 So the LORD God said to the serpent, "Because you have done this, cursed are you above all the livestock and all the wild animals! You will crawl on your belly and you will eat dust all the days of your life.*

Obviously, God was angry with Satan, and He dealt with him for his treachery. Then he tells Satan that he may have won the battle, but he did not win the war.

> *15 And I will put enmity between you and the woman, and between your offspring and hers; he will crush your head, and you will strike his heel." "NIV"*

God was declaring to Satan, and the world, that although Satan had struck a blow, He would defeat Satan. Just because he allowed Satan some freedom to operate, did not mean that God had given up control of the outcome.

By "crushing his head," God was declaring His final victory. Satan had caused the fall of man, but God would save them. This was the first prophecy concerning Jesus, the Christ.

What should be apparent is that God does not control us. He could, because He is all-powerful, but that is not how God operates. He is over Satan, but he allows Satan to function on his own. However, Satan must pay the consequences for his actions, just as we must. We all have choices to make. As you make yours, remember, eternity is a long time to spend regretting not making better decisions.

He tried to defeat Jesus through sin.

Satan knew that if Jesus sinned and was put to death, it would only atone, or pay the price for his sins alone. In order to atone for the sins of others, Jesus must be without sin.

To illustrate this point, think of two brothers, one guilty of a crime and the other innocent. The guilty one stands before the judge, and as sentence is passed, the innocent brother steps in and says, "Your honor, I know that a crime has been committed. I know that people have been hurt by it, and that restitution must be made. I know that you are a fair judge. You and I know that my brother committed the crime and deserves punishment, but I love my brother and I am willing to accept the punishment that he deserves. I ask that you let me to take his punishment and allow him to go free."

The judge could then respond in one of two ways depending on the guilt or innocence of the person asking the question:

"How can you, who are also guilty, hope to take the punishment of your brother, since you deserve punishment yourself? Request denied."

Alternatively, "Since you are innocent, it does not matter to me who is punished, you or your brother, as long as it satisfies the requirements of the law. If you are willing to die in his place, that is acceptable to me. I will do as you ask."

While this example shows what Jesus did for us, taking the punishment that we deserve, it would not have been possible unless Jesus himself was sinless.

Jesus endured many temptations.

Throughout his lifetime, Jesus was tempted, yet he remained sinless.

> *Luke 4:2-13*
>
> *2 where for forty days he was tempted by the devil. He ate nothing during those days, and at the end of them, he was hungry.*
>
> *3 The devil said to him, "If you are the Son of God, tell this stone to become bread."*
>
> *4 Jesus answered, "It is written: 'Man does not live on bread alone.'"*
>
> *5 The devil led him up to a high place and showed him in an instant all the kingdoms of the world. 6 And he said to him, "I will give you all their authority and splendor, for it has been given to me, and I can give it to anyone I want to. 7 So if you worship me, it will all be yours."*

> *8 Jesus answered, "It is written: 'Worship the Lord your God and serve him only.'"*
>
> *9 The devil led him to Jerusalem and had him stand on the highest point of the temple. "If you are the Son of God," he said, "throw yourself down from here. 10 For it is written:*
>
> *"'He will command his angels concerning you to guard you carefully; 11 they will lift you up in their hands, so that you will not strike your foot against a stone.'"*
>
> *12 Jesus answered, "It says: 'Do not put the Lord your God to the test.'"*
>
> *13 When the devil had finished all this tempting, he left him until an opportune time. "NIV"*

Satan would like us to think of Jesus as less than he is.

Only those who have not read the words of Jesus would think of him as just another messenger of God. He was not just a prophet or teacher. He claimed to be the Son of God. Not a watered-down version. Not "A" son, but "The" Son of God. Therefore, Jesus was who he claimed to be, or he was a false prophet.

However, his miracles proved he was who he claimed to be.

> *John 10:36-38*
>
> *Why then do you accuse me of blasphemy because I said, 'I am God's Son'? 37 Do not believe me unless I do what my Father does. 38 But if I do it, even though you do not believe me, believe the miracles, that you may know and understand that the Father is in me, and I in the Father." "NIV"*

John 14:11

11 Believe me when I say that I am in the Father and the Father is in me; or at least believe on the evidence of the miracles themselves. "NIV"

Satan sought to defeat God's plan through the death of Jesus.

Prophecy was fulfilled as Jesus quoted from the book of Zechariah written about 550 years before. His sheep were scattered.

Matt 26:31

31 Then Jesus told them, "This very night you will all fall away on account of me, for it is written:

"'I will strike the shepherd,

and the sheep of the flock will be scattered.' "NIV"

When Jesus was put to death, the sheep were scattered. These followers had lost their leader, and more than that, they questioned his leadership. Was Jesus really the Messiah? Was he really the anointed one who was to establish God's kingdom on earth? They thought he was and were willing to fight and even die for him. However, now to see him arrested, beaten, and put to death, just did not make sense. How could this happen to the one they have believed in?

But Jesus conquered Satan when he rose from the dead.

The greatest love was demonstrated when Jesus died for our sins. The greatest miracle was when he was resurrected from the grave.

1 Cor 15:3-8

3 For what I received I passed on to you as of first importance: that Christ died for our sins according to the Scriptures, 4 that he was buried, that he was raised on the third day according to the Scriptures, 5 and that he appeared to Peter, and then to the Twelve. 6 After that, he appeared to more than five hundred of the brothers at the same time, most of whom are still living, though some have fallen asleep. 7 Then he appeared to James, then to all the apostles, 8 and last of all he appeared to me also, "NIV"

This passage deserves further examination because it sums up the good news of Christ.

First, we see prophecy fulfilled:

▶ "Jesus died for our sins according to scripture"

▶ "Raised on the third day according to scripture"

Then we have several eyewitness accounts

▶ "He appeared to the twelve."

▶ He appeared to more than five hundred at the same time.

Of special note is that Paul includes "most of whom are still living," which indicates you can go speak to them and check out what I am saying.

▶ Then later, Jesus appeared to Paul, the author of much of the New Testament of the Bible. "As to one abnormally born."

Paul was not one of the original twelve apostles. He was not even an original follower of Jesus. In fact, Paul persecuted the followers until his personal experience with the risen Jesus, the Christ.

His sheep who were scattered became courageous.

On the day of Pentecost.

There is wonderful symbolism here. God has shown us the special relevance of Pentecost. Just as God uses prophesy to prove the validity of the Bible, He uses symbolism to reveal truth to us as one teaching builds on a former instruction.

> *Pentecost. A term derived from the Greek penteekostos, meaning fiftieth, which was applied to the fiftieth day after the Passover. It was the culmination of the feast of weeks (Ex 34:22; Deut 16:10), which began on the third day after the Passover with the presentation of the first harvest sheaves to God and which concluded with the offering of two loaves of unleavened bread*
>
> *Evangelical Dictionary of Theology. Copyright 1984 by Baker Books. All rights reserved. Used by permission.*

In the Bible, the number 7 represents perfection, or completeness. In this case, the festival of weeks, 7 days, is combined with 7 weeks. It is with emphasis that God shows us 7 x 7=49 and the next or 50th day is observed as Pentecost.

It began on the third day after Passover. Jesus was put to death on Passover and resurrected after three days. Drawing from the definition for Pentecost that we just looked at:

"Presentation of the first harvest." Jesus was the first of many to be resurrected.

"Unleavened bread" Unleavened means without yeast and is symbolic of without sin.

Let me sum it up this way. Jesus, who was without sin (unleavened bread) through his dying words, "it is finished" (completed), all that is necessary for our resurrection. As the first fruits (first harvest), he was the first to be resurrected into the family of God.

They received the Holy Spirit and began preaching the good news.

This was like no other day; like no other Pentecost! This was the day foretold by Jesus, when the Apostles would receive the Holy Spirit, and begin their mission of preaching the good news of Jesus to all people.

Acts 2:1-13

2:1 When the day of Pentecost came, they were all together in one place. 2 Suddenly a sound like the blowing of a violent wind came from heaven and filled the whole house where they were sitting. 3 They saw what seemed to be tongues of fire that separated and came to rest on each of them. 4 All of them were filled with the Holy Spirit and began to speak in other tongues as the Spirit enabled them.

By a miracle, each one heard in their own language.

> *5 Now there were staying in Jerusalem God-fearing Jews from every nation under heaven. 6 When they heard this sound, a crowd came together in bewilderment, because each one heard them speaking in his own language.*
>
> *7 Utterly amazed, they asked: "Are not all these men who are speaking Galileans? 8 Then how is it that each of us hears them in his own native language? 9 Parthians, Medes and Elamites; residents of Mesopotamia, Judea and Cappadocia, Pontus and*

> *Asia, 10 Phrygia and Pamphylia, Egypt and the parts of Libya near Cyrene; visitors from Rome 11(both Jews and converts to Judaism); Cretans and Arabs-we hear them declaring the wonders of God in our own tongues!" 12 Amazed and perplexed, they asked one another, "What does this mean?"*

Some who heard understood, and some did not.

> *13 Some, however, made fun of them and said, "They have had too much wine." "NIV"*

Therefore, the miracle was twofold. First, the text says they who were filled with the Spirit were able to speak in different tongues, or languages. Then it says some were amazed, while some made fun because they did not understand. One might surmise from this passage that if the Holy Spirit enabled the Apostles to speak in many different languages, it would have been in all languages. Moreover, since some heard and some did not, that also indicates that they were hearing by a miracle of the Holy Spirit. Those who did not understand did not receive the gift of the Spirit because their hearts were hardened.

Peter, who had denied Jesus at his trial, became bold.

Peter begins by stating that these people were eyewitnesses to the miracles performed by God through Jesus. Then he states this was according to God's purpose and we can believe because it is prophecy fulfilled.

> *Acts 2:22-38*
>
> *22 "Men of Israel, listen to this: Jesus of Nazareth was a man accredited by God to you by miracles, wonders and signs, which God did among you through him, as you yourselves know.*

> 23 This man was handed over to you by God's set purpose and foreknowledge; and you, with the help of wicked men, put him to death by nailing him to the cross. 24 But God raised him from the dead, freeing him from the agony of death, because it was impossible for death to keep its hold on him. 25 David said about him:
>
> "'I saw the Lord always before me. Because he is at my right hand, I will not be shaken. 26 Therefore my heart is glad and my tongue rejoices; my body also will live in hope, 27 because you will not abandon me to the grave, nor will you let your Holy One see decay. 28 You have made known to me the paths of life; you will fill me with joy in your presence.'
>
> 29 "Brothers, I can tell you confidently that the patriarch David died and was buried, and his tomb is here to this day. 30 But he was a prophet and knew that God had promised him on oath that he would place one of his descendants on his throne. 31 Seeing what was ahead, he spoke of the resurrection of the Christ, that he was not abandoned to the grave, nor did his body see decay.

Then Peter gives his own testimony about the resurrection, confirmed by others.

> 32 God has raised this Jesus to life, and we are all witnesses of the fact. 33 Exalted to the right hand of God, he has received from the Father the promised Holy Spirit and has poured out what you now see and hear. 34 For David did not ascend to heaven, and yet he said,

> "'The Lord said to my Lord: "Sit at my right hand 35 until I make your enemies a footstool for your feet."*

Concluding with Jesus is both Lord and Christ. Acknowledging this, you should repent and be baptized.

> *36 "Therefore let all Israel be assured of this: God has made this Jesus, whom you crucified, both Lord and Christ."*
>
> *37 When the people heard this, they were cut to the heart and said to Peter and the other apostles, "Brothers, what shall we do?"*
>
> *38 Peter replied, "Repent and be baptized, every one of you, in the name of Jesus Christ for the forgiveness of your sins. And you will receive the gift of the Holy Spirit. "NIV"*

Then Satan tried to eliminate his followers.

After the Apostles witnessed the resurrected Christ, they would not deny him even to save their own lives. Most of them suffered a martyr's death. Moreover, it was not just the Apostles; many followers were put to death because they would not renounce Jesus.

At first, Saul persecuted them.

Note that Saul's name was later changed to Paul.

> *Acts 7:59-8:3*
>
> *59 While they were stoning him, Stephen prayed, "Lord Jesus, receive my spirit." 60 Then he fell on his knees and cried out, "Lord, do not hold this sin against them." When he had said this, he fell asleep.*

> *8:1 And Saul was there, giving approval to his death. On that day, a great persecution broke out against the church at Jerusalem, and all except the apostles were scattered throughout Judea and Samaria. 2 Godly men buried Stephen and mourned deeply for him. 3 But Saul began to destroy the church. Going from house to house, he dragged off men and women and put them in prison. "NIV"*

Instead of silencing them, they preached the word wherever they went. This, to me at least, is further evidence that Jesus was resurrected. The people who had witnessed some of the miracles, or seen Jesus after his resurrection, would not deny their faith even if it meant imprisonment or death.

> *Acts 8:4-8*
>
> *4 Those who had been scattered preached the word wherever they went. 5 Philip went down to a city in Samaria and proclaimed the Christ there. 6 When the crowds heard Philip and saw the miraculous signs he did, they all paid close attention to what he said. 7 With shrieks, evil spirits came out of many, and many paralytics and cripples were healed. 8 So there was great joy in that city. "NIV"*

Yet, Saul became an Apostle.

▶ He gave up his position of prominence as a Pharisee.

▶ He declared all his righteous deeds were like filthy rags.

▶ He was compelled to preach the good news regardless of his circumstances.

▶ He was beaten, shipwrecked, imprisoned, faced with the punishment of death.

▶ He did not do it for material gain or comfort. He was a tentmaker.

He ran the race to the end, storing up for himself the crown ▶ in heaven.

▶ His writings make up much of the New Testament.

What happened to Saul? What was his life changing experience?

Acts 9:1-20

9:1 Meanwhile, Saul was still breathing out murderous threats against the Lord's disciples. He went to the high priest 2 and asked him for letters to the synagogues in Damascus, so that if he found any there who belonged to the Way, whether men or women, he might take them as prisoners to Jerusalem. 3 As he neared Damascus on his journey, suddenly a light from heaven flashed around him. 4 He fell to the ground and heard a voice say to him, "Saul, Saul, why do you persecute me?"

5 "Who are you, Lord?" Saul asked.

"I am Jesus, whom you are persecuting," he replied. 6 "Now get up and go into the city, and you will be told what you must do."

7 The men traveling with Saul stood there speechless; they heard the sound but did not see anyone. 8 Saul got up from the ground, but when he opened his eyes he could see nothing. So they led him by the hand into Damascus. 9 For three days he was blind, and did not eat or drink anything.

10 In Damascus there was a disciple named Ananias. The Lord called to him in a vision, "Ananias!"

"Yes, Lord," he answered.

11 The Lord told him, "Go to the house of Judas on Straight Street and ask for a man from Tarsus named Saul, for he is praying. 12 In a vision he has seen a man named Ananias come and place his hands on him to restore his sight."

13 "Lord," Ananias answered, "I have heard many reports about this man and all the harm he has done to your saints in Jerusalem. 14 And he has come here with authority from the chief priests to arrest all who call on your name."

15 But the Lord said to Ananias, "Go! This man is my chosen instrument to carry my name before the Gentiles and their kings and before the people of Israel. 16 I will show him how much he must suffer for my name."

17 Then Ananias went to the house and entered it. Placing his hands on Saul, he said, "Brother Saul, the Lord-Jesus, who appeared to you on the road as you were coming here-has sent me so that you may see again and be filled with the Holy Spirit." 18 Immediately, something like scales fell from Saul's eyes, and he could see again. He got up and was baptized, 19 and after taking some food, he regained his strength.

Saul spent several days with the disciples in Damascus. 20 At once he began to preach in the synagogues that Jesus is the Son of God. "NIV"

This man Saul, whose name was changed to Paul, began his life in obedience to God, yet later called all his righteous works, worthless. Instead, he found a righteousness that comes by faith, apart from works.

Satan uses deception to confuse us and separate us from God.

As we have seen, many religions and belief systems have their own scripture. Some of these so-called sacred writings are of dubious origin. Others may appear to contain some truth, but have many errors and contradictions proving they are not inspired by God.

He appears as an angel of light, and his servants as servants of righteousness.

As you reflect on what we have covered, consider this. Muslims, Jehovah's Witnesses, Mormons, and Christian Scientists have things in common. All believe the Bible to be the word of God up to a point. Each believes they have received new revelations from God that takes precedence over the Bible. They have either rewritten the Bible, or added their own scripture, to be used for interpretation when studying the Bible or both. Where there are differences, they say the Bible is in error.

To that group we can add Roman Catholicism. They believe the pope, or Holy Father, is God's representative on earth. They add to the Bible what is termed as *tradition*. However, as we saw in the chapter on Roman Catholicism, they seem to overlook passages within the Bible that disagree with their teachings.

Each claim to be the one true faith, inspired by God, yet they are extremely different in their beliefs. For example, Muslims believe in one God. Catholics, as do other Christians, believe in One God who displays Himself in three persons. Jehovah's Witnesses believe that Jesus was first Michael the Archangel, and was a mighty God, but not the God Almighty. Mormons believe that God was first a man like us, and that one-day we can become a God like Him. While Christian Scientists believe they are God.

Muslims, as well as most Christians, believe in hell, while Jehovah's Witnesses and Christian Scientists do not. Catholics believe in heaven and hell but have added purgatory, a place where we will be punished for our unforgiven sins before we can enter heaven. Mormons believe that evil people will spend some time in hell, but there is an end to it and that at some point, all but a handful will all enter heaven. Nevertheless, as we saw in the chapter on Jehovah's Witnesses, the Bible tells us hell is real and we should fear it.

It should be obvious they cannot all be right. So how can we know what to believe? Many have faced this same question and decided to rely on the Bible alone. They test everything against it because they know people can be deceived and may mislead us. As the following passage illustrates, if an angel visited anyone, who discredited the Bible and introduced false teachings, it might well have been Satan, because the Bible tells us:

2 Cor 11:14-15

14 And no wonder, for Satan himself masquerades as an angel of light. 15 It is not surprising, then, if his servants masquerade as servants of righteousness. "NIV"

The most convincing liars just distort the truth or mix their lies with something believable. Satan is known as the father of lies, so he is the best at it. He says, believe the Bible to a point, but doubt its authenticity; believe me instead.

Satan deceives us through false prophets.

As we have seen, certain religions claim to be led by modern day prophets, but they have been discredited. It has been demonstrated that we can believe the Bible and we must be on guard for those who would deceive us.

Matt 24:11

11 and many false prophets will appear and deceive many people. "NIV"

In each instance, Satan brings the Bible into question and introduces something he says is better; a direct revelation from God, followed by a promise of continuing revelation. Yet, prophecy fulfilled, and symbolism like Pentecost, prove the Bible can be trusted as the word of God. Nobody else can make such claims about their scripture.

Satan attacks his followers from within.

Jesus taught us with parables. In one instance, he spoke of Satan as an enemy who sowed weeds among good seed. This could be likened to mixing lies with the truth, producing followers who appear like the real thing, but in the end, they have different destinies.

Matt 13:24-30

24 Jesus told them another parable: "The kingdom of heaven is like a man who sowed good seed in his field. 25 But while everyone was sleeping, his enemy came and sowed weeds among the wheat, and went away. 26 When the wheat sprouted and formed heads, then the weeds also appeared.

27 "The owner's servants came to him and said, 'Sir, didn't you sow good seed in your field? Where then did the weeds come from?'

28 "'An enemy did this,' he replied.

"The servants asked him, 'Do you want us to go and pull them up?'

> 29 "'No,' he answered, 'because while you are pulling the weeds, you may root up the wheat with them. 30 Let both grow together until the harvest. At that time I will tell the harvesters: First collect the weeds and tie them in bundles to be burned; then gather the wheat and bring it into my barn.'" "NIV"

Sad but true, not everyone identifying themselves as Christians, really are.

Not everyone who attends a place of worship is a true believer, just as going into your garage does not make you a car.

> Matt 7:22-23
>
> 22 At the Judgment many will tell me, 'Lord, Lord, we told others about you and used your name to cast out demons and to do many other great miracles.' 23 But I will reply, 'You have never been mine. Go away, for your deeds are evil.' "TLB"

This passage could be aimed at hypocrites, those that speak one way, and live another. On the other hand, it could relate to people who attend church on a regular basis, but never really know why. Let me give you a few examples:

I have been to islands where missionaries established a church. Their aim was to share the good news of Jesus. They built places of worship and to this day, the people dress in white every Sunday and attend these churches. Yet, this seems more of a tradition than a religious exercise.

However, you do not have to go to an island to see the same phenomenon. The perception of most people is that God keeps track of our good and bad deeds. If our good outweighs the bad, we will be admitted to heaven. Some think that by attending church you score points with God. They do not understand what God desires from us. They place their faith in themselves rather than in Jesus. While there are many good reasons for attending a place of worship, just showing up is not one of them.

Confusing many others into believing that all paths lead to God.

Obviously, as has been demonstrated, the notion that all paths lead to God is false.

Today, Hinduism has become an all embracing, all-encompassing way of life. The "whatever works for you," attitude and "all paths lead to God" philosophy, may sound nice, but it simply cannot be true. While it may avoid confrontations and seems non-judgmental, it should be obvious to all that many paths do not lead to God.

The origin of Hinduism is unknown, and therefore unreliable. Yet, it became the basis for many other religions or belief systems. It began as polytheistic, teaching that there are many gods, yet the beliefs that followed vary greatly in what they teach about God. Monism, Pantheism, Henotheism, are vastly different concepts. It seems that over time, people have designed their own version of God. Rather than favoring one belief over another, they try to be all-inclusive. However, they cannot all be right. Considering the source, and evolution of beliefs, it is more likely that none of these theories are right. After all, what are they based on?

Actually, these beliefs did not originate with Hinduism they have just been repackaged. They go back to the beginning of time. The author of the "many ways to God" is Satan, the father of lies. He is the great deceiver. His goal is to separate us from God either by confusing or distracting us.

Jesus said,

> Matt 7:13-15
>
> 13 "Enter by the narrow gate; for wide is the gate and broad is the way that leads to destruction, and there are many who go in by it. 14 Because narrow is the gate and difficult is the way which leads to life, and there are few who find it.
>
> 15 "Beware of false prophets, who come to you in sheep's clothing, but inwardly they are ravenous wolves. "NKJV"

Taking another look at this chart, do you now see what Jesus was telling us?

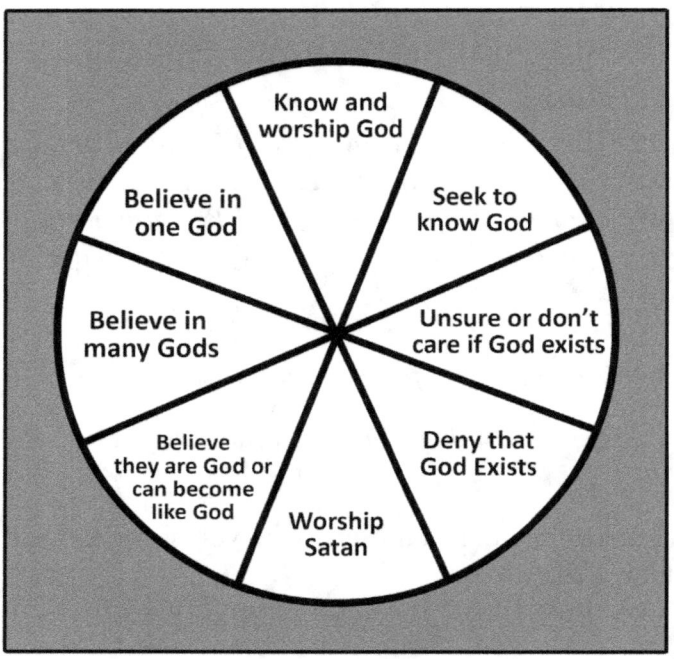

Satan wins whenever he diverts our attention from the one way to God. Seeking to please God is not enough; just as seeking to know God, is not the same as knowing and worshiping Him. As Jesus tells us:

John 14:6

6 Jesus answered, "I am the way and the truth and the life. No one comes to the Father except through me. "NIV"

Dear friends, the Bible is so clear, do not be deceived.

1 John 4:1-3

4:1 Dear friends, do not believe every spirit, but test the spirits to see whether they are from God, because many false prophets have gone out into the world. 2

This is how you can recognize the Spirit of God: Every spirit that acknowledges that Jesus Christ has come in the flesh is from God, 3 but every spirit that does not acknowledge Jesus is not from God. This is the spirit of the antichrist, which you have heard is coming and even now is already in the world. "NIV"

It does matter to God what you believe.

The next section is all about God. He wants you to know Him and your relationship to Him. Following that is an invitation, and a warning that your decision has eternal consequences.

Section VIII

Knowing and worshiping God

God expects our worship, an expression of love. However, before we can truly worship God, we must learn about Him.

The God of the Bible is:

***Omnipotent;* all powerful.**

He created everything; therefore, God is over all and can do anything.

Col 1:16-17

16 For by Him all things were created that are in heaven and that are on earth, visible and invisible, whether thrones or dominions or principalities or powers. All things were created through Him and for Him. 17 And He is before all things, and in Him all things consist. "NKJV"

Whenever you become amazed at the discoveries of man, remember, before man found it God made it, and before man created it, God created man.

Moreover, His mighty power over the elements was displayed with the several plagues as recorded in the book of Exodus. He brought them on Egypt in order to convince the Pharaoh to free the Hebrew slaves. However, His purpose was even greater. He wanted to reveal Himself to a confused world and declare that He is the one and only LORD.

> Ex 10:1-2
>
> *10:1 Then the LORD said to Moses, "Go to Pharaoh, for I have hardened his heart and the hearts of his officials so that I may perform these miraculous signs of mine among them 2 that you may tell your children and grandchildren how I dealt harshly with the Egyptians and how I performed my signs among them, and that you may know that I am the LORD." "NIV"*

He is sovereign.

> *Sovereignty of God, A term by which is expressed the supreme rulership of God. This is rightly held to be not an attribute of God but a prerogative based upon the perfections of the divine Being.*
>
> *(From The New Unger's Bible Dictionary. Originally published by Moody Press of Chicago, Illinois. Copyright (c) 1988.)*

The key thing to understand here is that as an all-powerful God, He can do anything He wishes. However, that does not make him all controlling. As our sovereign LORD, it is His prerogative to intervene in our lives or not. Let me illustrate:

Let us first acknowledge that God created everything, including what we often refer to as *nature*. With the right weather conditions, we can predict a storm is coming. These storms can be for our benefit. There is a saying where I come from that "March winds, followed by April showers, bring May flowers."

On the other hand, sometimes weather patterns are severe. We could have droughts or floods, calm seas, or hurricanes, or even earthquakes and tsunamis. While God could control these things if He chose to, we usually find that He lets nature take its course. In fact, that is the way He designed it, like the rest of our ecosystem.

Some people would like to believe that severe weather is a result of God's wrath. While there are some instances recorded in the Bible to substantiate the fact that He can exercise His control over nature, they are rare. An example from scripture:

Matt 5:43-46

44 But I tell you: Love your enemies and pray for those who persecute you, 45 that you may be sons of your Father in heaven. He causes his sun to rise on the evil and the good, and sends rain on the righteous and the unrighteous. "NIV"

Some have concluded that since God is over all, He controls every aspect of our lives. While I believe He can intervene whenever He chooses to, I strongly disagree with the notion that He controls us. This is discussed further later in this section.

Omniscient; **knowing all.**

Let us look at two variations on this theme. God knows all. When scientists boast about their discoveries, remember that He created the things to be discovered.

Nothing is hidden from Him. He knows everything we do. Moreover, He knows us better than we know ourselves.

Omnipresent; **everywhere at once, or always with us.**

We are limited, but God is not. This is not to say that God is in everything as in the belief of pantheism. His Spirit can be everywhere at once, but that does not mean dwelling within every object of nature.

Understanding the Trinity

The *Trinity,* one God who manifests Himself as three persons: Father, Son and Holy Spirit, is difficult for many people to comprehend. Yet, this is vital in order to really understand God and be grateful for how He demonstrates His love for us. To gain an appreciation, let us start at the beginning with the first verse in the Bible.

Gen 1:1

1:1 In the beginning God created the heavens and the earth. "NIV"

To get a better understanding, we will look at the word for God used in this verse, as it was written in the original Hebrew language.

OT: 430

'elohiym (el-o-heem'); plural of OT: 433; gods in the ordinary sense; but specifically used (in the plural thus, especially with the article) of the supreme God;

(Biblesoft's New Exhaustive Strong's Numbers and Concordance with Expanded Greek-Hebrew Dictionary. Copyright (c) 1994, Biblesoft and International Bible Translators, Inc.)

So we see that elohiym is not a name. Rather, it is descriptive of the supreme God, who is plural in nature. With this understanding, the following verse makes sense. Otherwise, the following verse would appear odd. At first glance it would appear that *God*, singular, combined with *"Let us make man in our,"* in the plural.

Gen 1:26

26 Then God (elohiym, in the plural) said, "Let us make man in our image, in our likeness, and let them rule over the fish of the sea and the birds of the air, over the livestock, over all the earth, and over all the creatures that move along the ground." "NIV"

Elohiym also refers to those who are in the position to judge, as gods. In the following verse, Jesus quotes Psalm 82:6 as he answers those who wanted to stone him to death for saying he was God's Son.

John 10:34-38

34 Jesus answered them, "Is it not written in your Law, 'I have said you are gods'? (Judges) 35 If he called them 'gods,' to whom the word of God came-and the Scripture cannot be broken- 36 what about the one whom the Father set apart as his very own and sent into the world? Why then do you accuse me of blasphemy because I said, 'I am God's Son'? 37 Do not believe me unless I do what my Father does. 38 But if I do it, even though you do not believe me, believe the miracles, that you may know and understand that the Father is in me, and I in the Father." "NIV"

Examples of the Trinity in scripture.

In this verse, we see the Father, Son and Holy Spirit all gathered at one place in time.

Matt 3:16-17

16 As soon as Jesus was baptized, he went up out of the water. At that moment heaven was opened, and he saw the Spirit of God descending like a dove and lighting on him. 17 And a voice from heaven said, "This is my Son, whom I love; with him I am well pleased." "NIV"

Luke 10:21

21 At that time Jesus, full of joy through the Holy Spirit, said, "I praise you, Father, Lord of heaven and earth, "NIV"

Here is another example when Jesus said when he went away the counselor, or Holy Spirit, would come.

John 15:26

26 "When the Counselor comes, whom I will send to you from the Father, the Spirit of truth who goes out from the Father, he will testify about me. "NIV"

The Father

The designation of Father indicates the type of relationship God would like to have with us. There is more on this throughout this book and especially in the section on Confucianism, including when Jesus instructed us on the prayer that begins, "Our Father in heaven."

The Father is Spirit.

John 4:21-24

21 Jesus declared, ... true worshipers will worship the Father in spirit and truth, for they are the kind of worshipers the Father seeks. 24 God is spirit, and his worshipers must worship in spirit and in truth." "NIV"

He is God, apart from us, remaining undefiled, Holy, and pure.

In fact, nothing that is impure can encounter God, our Father. In the Old Testament, even the priests were required to go through ceremonial cleansing and give offerings to atone for their sins before they were fit to enter into the Holy of Holies. This was the innermost part of the Temple, where the "Ark of the Covenant" was kept. If anyone entered who had not gone through a purification process, they died on the spot.

Over all.

He is over all, you, me, and everything else, whether you accept that fact yet or not. As you will see, even the Son and the Holy Spirit are subservient to the Father.

He is jealous.

Since the beginning, God has desired a relationship with us. Nevertheless, to be of value, the relationship has to be one of choice. We are not forced to accept Him, but he is angered when we reject Him. This is a major theme of the Bible and is emphasized repeatedly.

He wants a relationship with us as our Father.

The Bible is filled with passages declaring this truth. There is a vivid word picture brought to mind with the story of the prodigal son. Jesus taught about the love of our Father in heaven as he related the story about a son who had broken the relationship with his father, which was later restored.

> *Luke 15:11-32*
>
> *11 Jesus continued: "There was a man who had two sons. 12 The younger one said to his father, 'Father, give me my share of the estate.' So he divided his property between them.*
>
> *13 "Not long after that, the younger son got together all he had, set off for a distant country and there squandered his wealth in wild living. 14 After he had spent everything, there was a severe famine in that whole country, and he began to be in need. 15 So he went and hired himself out to a citizen of that country, who sent him to his fields to feed pigs. 16 He longed to fill his stomach with the pods that the pigs were eating, but no one gave him anything.*
>
> *17 "When he came to his senses, he said, 'How many of my father's hired men have food to spare, and here I am starving to death! 18 I will set out and go back to my father and say to him: Father, I have sinned against heaven and against you. 19 I am no longer worthy to be called your son; make me like one of your hired men.' 20 So he got up and went to his father.*
>
> *"But while he was still a long way off, his father saw*

him and was filled with compassion for him; he ran to his son, threw his arms around him and kissed him.

21 "The son said to him, 'Father, I have sinned against heaven and against you. I am no longer worthy to be called your son.'

22 "But the father said to his servants, 'Quick! Bring the best robe and put it on him. Put a ring on his finger and sandals on his feet. 23 Bring the fattened calf and kill it. Let's have a feast and celebrate. 24 For this son of mine was dead and is alive again; he was lost and is found.' So they began to celebrate.

25 "Meanwhile, the older son was in the field. When he came near the house, he heard music and dancing. 26 So he called one of the servants and asked him what was going on. 27 'Your brother has come,' he replied, 'and your father has killed the fattened calf because he has him back safe and sound.'

28 "The older brother became angry and refused to go in. So his father went out and pleaded with him. 29 But he answered his father, 'Look! All these years I've been slaving for you and never disobeyed your orders. Yet you never gave me even a young goat so I could celebrate with my friends. 30 But when this son of yours who has squandered your property with prostitutes comes home, you kill the fattened calf for him!'

31 "'My son,' the father said, 'you are always with me, and everything I have is yours. 32 But we had to celebrate and be glad, because this brother of yours was dead and is alive again; he was lost and is found.'"
"NIV"

Picture that. God loves us so much that he allows us to wander wherever we desire. He does not impose His will upon us. It is our choice to accept fellowship with Him or reject it. In spite of what we have done or how we have lived our lives, even if we have been far from Him, he eagerly awaits our restored relationship.

The Son.

Jesus often referred to himself as the Son of Man. He was conceived of a virgin by the power of the Holy Spirit, becoming both God and Man.

Immanuel; God with us.

Matthew was quoting Isaiah who had prophesied hundreds of years earlier.

> *Matt 1:21-23*
>
> *21 She will give birth to a son, and you are to give him the name Jesus, because he will save his people from their sins."*
>
> *22 All this took place to fulfill what the Lord had said through the prophet: 23 "The virgin will be with child and will give birth to a son, and they will call him Immanuel"-which means, "God with us." "NIV"*

Mary was told that she would give birth to the Son of God yet remain a virgin.

> *Luke 1:31,34-35,37*
>
> *31 You will be with child and give birth to a son, and you are to give him the name Jesus. 32 He will be great and will be called the Son of the Most High.*

> *34 "How will this be," Mary asked the angel, "since I am a virgin?"*
>
> *35 The angel answered, "The Holy Spirit will come upon you, and the power of the Most High will overshadow you. So the holy one to be born will be called the Son of God.*
>
> *37 For nothing is impossible with God." "NIV"*

Jesus was the One and only who came from the Father.

> *John 1:14,18*
>
> *14 The Word became flesh and made his dwelling among us. We have seen his glory, the glory of the One and Only, who came from the Father, full of grace and truth.*
>
> *18 No one has ever seen God, but God the One and Only, who is at the Father's side, has made him known. "NIV"*

Note that in verse 18, John was speaking of Jesus as God, who returned to the Father after his resurrection. Unlike the rest of us whose spirits were formed within us (see Zech 12:1 in the Bible and the section on Mormonism), he was indwelt with the spirit of God.

> *John 14:9-11*
>
> *9 Jesus replied, "Don't you even yet know who I am, Philip, even after all this time I have been with you? Anyone who has seen me has seen the Father! So why are you asking to see him? 10 Don't you believe that I am in the Father and the Father is in me? The words I say are not my own but are from my Father who lives in me. And he does his work through me. 11 Just believe*

> it-that I am in the Father and the Father is in me. Or else believe it because of the mighty miracles you have seen me do. "TLB"

Unlike the Father who is spirit alone, Jesus has a body of flesh and bones.

Even after his resurrection, Jesus appeared to many in bodily form, including his apostles.

> Luke 24:37-39
>
> 37 But they were startled and frightened and thought that they were seeing a spirit. 38 And He said to them, "Why are you troubled, and why do doubts arise in your hearts? 39 "See My hands and My feet, that it is I Myself; touch Me and see, for a spirit does not have flesh and bones as you see that I have." "NIV"

He performed miracles proving he was the Son of God.

There are numerous accounts in the Bible of people who were miraculously healed by Jesus. Yet, he did not do it for his own glory. In fact, many times he instructed the person he had just healed to tell no one. Other times, he performed miracles so that people might believe he was the Son of God. Numerous passages can be found in the section on Buddhism, although these are only samples of the many he healed.

> **John 14:11**
>
> **11 Believe me when I say that I am in the Father and the Father is in me; or at least believe on the evidence of the miracles themselves. "NIV"**

He declares the Father is greater.

John 14:28-29

28 "You heard me say, 'I am going away and I am coming back to you.' If you loved me, you would be glad that I am going to the Father, for the Father is greater than I. "NIV"

Why would God have a Son?

We looked at this in the section on Judaism and Islam. One reason for God to take a body of flesh and bones and become like us is so that we can relate to him. As we have seen, God the Father is spirit. He is Holy and pure and unapproachable. However, through His Son, we have access to God. We can come near Him. Jesus has many names in the Bible that are descriptive, for example:

The Good Shepherd: Jesus would give his life to save his flock. He would leave the ninety-nine to search for and save the one lost sheep.

Teacher: Jesus brought the scriptures to life, instructing his followers, confounding his learned critics, and rebuking Satan.

Physician: Healing many including those born lame and blind, he also brought the dead back to life. As we discussed in the section on Buddhism, He had compassion on those he encountered. Many times Jesus would heal someone and instruct them to tell no one.

The Lamb of God: When the time came, Jesus was offered up as a sacrifice to God. His blood was shed as our "Passover Lamb." As we saw in the section on Judaism, he is our scapegoat, thus satisfying the requirements of the law for those who place their trust in him.

He experienced life as we have.

There is another reason that God had a Son who became like us; so He can relate. This was the reason he emptied Himself. As God Omnipotent, He was all-powerful and as Omniscient, He knew all. With these attributes, it would not be difficult to live a perfect sinless life. However, as someone who emptied himself, or laid aside these attributes, living and experiencing life as we have, he is more inclined to have compassion on us. At the same time, we are without excuse before Him.

When the time comes and you are standing before God, and He asks you, "Why should I let you into my heaven?" You will not be able to say, "Well God, I know I wasn't perfect, but you don't know what it was like for me."

Although God, he emptied himself, being made in the likeness of men.

Phil 2:6-8

6 who, although He existed in the form of God, did not regard equality with God a thing to be grasped, 7 but emptied himself, taking the form of a bond-servant, and being made in the likeness of men. 8 Being found in appearance as a man, He humbled Himself by becoming obedient to the point of death, even death on a cross. "NASU"

Jesus, as the Son of God, had a special purpose that was determined in the Garden of Eden when Adam and Eve sinned. It appeared that Lucifer had brought the downfall of all mankind, but God declared He would prevail. He would bring about the salvation of man by providing forgiveness through Jesus Christ.

Rom 5:12-13

12 When Adam sinned, sin entered the entire human race. His sin spread death throughout all the world, so everything began to grow old and die, for all sinned. "TLB"

Rom 5:15

For this one man, Adam, brought death to many through his sin. But this one man, Jesus Christ, brought forgiveness to many through God's mercy. "TLB"

He did not know all things when *incarnate*, or as he was in the flesh.

He prayed to the Father, communing with Him for instruction.

John 12:49

49 For I did not speak of my own accord, but the Father who sent me commanded me what to say and how to say it. "NIV"

When asked about the end times and his second coming Jesus said only the Father knows.

Mark 13:32

32 "No one knows about that day or hour, not even the angels in heaven, nor the Son, but only the Father. "NIV"

He does the will of the Father.

John 14:31

31 but the world must learn that I love the Father and that I do exactly what my Father has commanded me. "NIV"

He submits to the will of the Father, even unto death.

On the night before his arrest and execution, Jesus was tormented by the thought of how he must suffer and die.

> Luke 22:42-44
>
> 42 *"Father, if you are willing, take this cup from me; yet not my will, but yours be done." 43 An angel from heaven appeared to him and strengthened him. 44 And being in anguish, he prayed more earnestly, and his sweat was like drops of blood falling to the ground.* "NIV"

This was last and greatest temptation of Christ. He did not fear death because he knew that he would be resurrected on the third day. What caused him to be in such anguish as to sweat drops of blood was his fearful expectation of being tortured to death. First, to be beaten with bones and rocks affixed to strips of leather, stripping the flesh from his body as he was whipped. Next, he was to suffer being crucified.

First having his hands and feet nailed to a cross, then placing it upright into the ground so that he would hang in an upright position as he was left to suffer and die. As it fell into position, the jolt was enough to pull his arms out of socket by the weight of his body. This painful form of execution, crucifixion, is where we get the word *excruciating* to describe intense pain. To get a sense of how he suffered think of this. At the ends of the wrists and in the ankles are nerve centers. If you have ever hit your "crazy bone" and felt an immediate pain shoot through your whole arm, you might imagine what it was like for Christ. Driving nails into these nerve centers was bad enough but in order to breathe in that position, hanging from the cross, he had to pull himself up by his hands and push with his ankles. This process intensified the pain, and it took hours for him to die.

With these fearful expectations, Jesus was probably recalling his earlier temptation by the devil. How he could avoid the pain and suffering that was to come, and still be ruler of the world if he would turn from the Father and worship Satan.

> *Luke 4:5-8*
>
> *5 The devil led him up to a high place and showed him in an instant all the kingdoms of the world. 6 And he said to him, "I will give you all their authority and splendor, for it has been given to me, and I can give it to anyone I want to. 7 So if you worship me, it will all be yours."*
>
> *8 Jesus answered, "It is written: 'Worship the Lord your God and serve him only.'" "NIV"*

Nevertheless, Jesus remained pure and innocent, submitting to the will of the Father even unto a terrible death. There were reasons for this and some especially important points to understand.

▶ It was possible for Jesus to sin; otherwise, the offer by Satan would not have been considered a temptation.

▶ If Jesus had ever sinned, he could not have died for our sins. Since the wages of sin is death, if he had sinned, he would only have died for his own sins.

▶ It had to be a horrible painful death to atone for the sins of anyone, even the most evil person who ever lived.

▶ Nobody should ever think that the blood of Jesus could not atone for their sins, no matter what they have done. Nor should they feel that way about others.

However, Jesus did not suffer and die, receiving the

punishment for everyone, but only for whosoever believes. There is more on this subject a little later.

Jesus will judge us.

> *John 5:22-23*
>
> *22 Moreover, the Father judges no one, but has entrusted all judgment to the Son, 23 that all may honor the Son just as they honor the Father. "NIV"*

Being our judge honors Jesus, yet he judges to please his Father, the one who sent him.

> *John 5:30*
>
> *30 By myself I can do nothing; I judge only as I hear, and my judgment is just, for I seek not to please myself but him who sent me. "NIV"*

Jesus judges as only he can.

In his unique position as "Son of God," and "Son of Man," he can relate to us in our weaknesses to a Holy God. On the other hand, we will find ourselves kneeling before a Holy God without any excuses for our sins.

There is more on judgment, justice and mercy discussed a little later.

Jesus is Lord!

One day every knee will bow and tongue confess; either here, or hereafter.

> *Phil 2:9-11*
>
> *Therefore God exalted him to the highest place and gave him the name that is above every name, that at the*

name of Jesus every knee should bow, in heaven and on earth and under the earth, and every tongue confess that Jesus Christ is Lord. "NIV"

Here and elsewhere, emphasis is placed on the name of "Jesus." It is not magical. In fact, as discussed earlier, Jesus is the Greek translation for Yeshua, from the Hebrew, as is Joshua from the Hebrew to English. It was not an uncommon name, meaning "God Saves." The emphasis should be on "name," which refers to the power and authority.

The Holy Spirit.

The Holy Spirit is not like the Father, nor the Son, but is still one of the three manifestations of God. To help our understanding, let us look at the definitions of the words in their original language as written in the Bible.

Holy Spirit

The Hebrew word for "spirit" (ruwach) can also mean wind, breath, or life-force. Most commonly designated as "of God" or "of the Lord," the Spirit appears as God's agent of creation (Gen 1:2; Job 33:4; 34:14-15), a mode of his interacting with humans. Evangelical Dictionary of Biblical Theology. Copyright 1996 by Baker Books. All rights reserved. Used by permission.

See also, God, 'elohiym, as illustrated earlier in "Understanding the Trinity".

With this understanding of the words for Spirit and of God, as written in the original Hebrew, we get a better understanding of the first passages in the Bible, and of the Trinity.

Gen 1:1-2

1:1 In the beginning God ('elohiym) created the

heavens and the earth. 2 Now the earth was formless and empty, darkness was over the surface of the deep, and the Spirit (ruwach) of God ('elohiym) was hovering over the waters. "NIV"

We can see the Trinity demonstrated again by this passage. Jesus, indwelt by the spirit of God, breathed on his disciples to give them the Holy Spirit.

John 20:21-22

21 Again Jesus said, "Peace be with you! As the Father has sent me, I am sending you." 22 And with that he breathed on them and said, "Receive the Holy Spirit. "NIV"

The Spirit is also subservient to the Father.

John 16:13

13 But when he, the Spirit of truth, comes, he will guide you into all truth. He will not speak on his own; he will speak only what he hears, "NIV"

The Holy Spirit interacts with us as our councilor or comforter.

Unlike the Father who remains holy and pure at a distance from us, and nothing like Jesus who is uniquely both God and a man like us, the Holy Spirit interacts with us. In fact, the Bible says the Spirit fills us. Some examples are:

Acts 4:8

8 Then Peter, filled with the Holy Spirit, said to them: "NIV"

Acts 4:31

31 After they prayed, the place where they were meeting was shaken. And they were all filled with the Holy Spirit and spoke the word of God boldly. "NIV"

Acts 9:17-18

17 Then Ananias went to the house and entered it. Placing his hands on Saul, he said, "Brother Saul, the Lord-Jesus, who appeared to you on the road as you were coming here-has sent me so that you may see again and be filled with the Holy Spirit." "NIV"

Acts 13:9

9 Then Saul, who was also called Paul, filled with the Holy Spirit, "NIV"

Acts 13:52

52 And the disciples were filled with joy and with the Holy Spirit. "NIV"

The work of the Holy Spirit.

Just before his death, Jesus told us that he would send the Counselor and gives us an indication of his work.

John 16:7-11

Unless I go away, the Counselor will not come to you; but if I go, I will send him to you. 8 When he comes, he will convict the world of guilt in regard to sin and righteousness and judgment: 9 in regard to sin, because men do not believe in me; 10 in regard to righteousness, because I am going to the Father, where you can see me no longer; 11 and in regard to judgment, because the prince of this world now stands condemned. "NIV"

At Pentecost, there was a demonstration to both show the people that the Holy Spirit had indeed come and of His miraculous ability to work through others in sharing the good news of Jesus Christ.

> *Acts 2:1-4*
>
> *2:1 When the day of Pentecost came, they were all together in one place. 2 Suddenly a sound like the blowing of a violent wind came from heaven and filled the whole house where they were sitting. 3 They saw what seemed to be tongues of fire that separated and came to rest on each of them. 4 All of them were filled with the Holy Spirit and began to speak in other tongues as the Spirit enabled them. "NIV"*

He directs the speech of the believers.

> *1 Cor 2:13*
>
> *13 This is what we speak, not in words taught us by human wisdom but in words taught by the Spirit, expressing spiritual truths in spiritual words. "NIV"*

He knows us better than we know ourselves and even prays to the Father for us. I like the way the Living Bible describes this.

> *Rom 8:26-28*
>
> *26 And in the same way-by our faith --the Holy Spirit helps us with our daily problems and in our praying. For we don't even know what we should pray for nor how to pray as we should, but the Holy Spirit prays for us with such feeling that it cannot be expressed in words. 27 And the Father who knows all hearts knows, of course, what the Spirit is saying as he pleads for us in harmony with God's own will. 28 And we know that*

all that happens to us is working for our good if we love God and are fitting into his plans. "TLB"

The Bible tells us that sanctification is the work of the Holy Spirit. This will be discussed in detail a little later in this section.

Understanding our relationship to God

One of the keys to understanding our relationship is thinking about how we view our position. Do we see ourselves at a distance from God, or nearness? Do we see God as unapproachable and unknowable? He neither hears our prayers, nor is interested in our lives. Or do we seek a relationship with God and would like to think he hears our prayers and, subject to his will, answers them. What about heaven and hell?

God is over all.

Whether you chose to accept that fact or not, eventually, you will acknowledge that God is over all. It will either be here while there is time, or hereafter when it is too late. The Bible tells us:

Prov 9:10

10 The fear of the LORD is the beginning of wisdom, "NAS"

Fearing God means having a respect for who He is and what He has done.

To gain a better understanding of what is meant by "the fear of" in this and other passages we look at the interpretation of what was written in the original Hebrew.

> OT: 3372
>
> *yare' (yaw-ray'); a primitive root; to fear; morally, to revere; cause. to frighten:*
>
> *KJV - affright, be (make) afraid, dread (-ful), (put in) fear (-ful, -fully, -ing), (be had in) reverence (-end), X see, terrible (act, -ness, thing).*
>
> *(Biblesoft's New Exhaustive Strong's Numbers and Concordance with Expanded Greek-Hebrew Dictionary. Copyright (c) 1994, Biblesoft and International Bible Translators, Inc.)*

It is interesting to consider that we could come to a point of so revering God that we would be fearful of separation from Him. Alternatively, we may be so in awe of Him that we have a fearful expectation of what He might do to us if we do not do His will.

In the first place, we see that those who fear God and revere, or hold Him in the highest regard, are now in a position to relate to Him and He with them, as illustrated by the following passages.

> Ps 85:9
>
> 9 Surely his salvation is near those who fear him," NIV"
>
> Ps 25:14
>
> 14 The LORD confides in those who fear him;
>
> he makes his covenant known to them. "NIV"

God loves those who worship Him and put their trust and hope in Him.

Ps 33:18-22

18 But the eyes of the LORD are on those who fear him, on those whose hope is in his unfailing love, 19 to deliver them from death and keep them alive in famine.

20 We wait in hope for the LORD; he is our help and our shield. 21 In him our hearts rejoice, for we trust in his holy name. 22 May your unfailing love rest upon us, O LORD, even as we put our hope in you. "NIV"

Ps 147:11

11 the LORD delights in those who fear him, who put their hope in his unfailing love. "NIV"

He has compassion on those who fear Him.

Ps 103:11-13

11 For as high as the heavens are above the earth, so great is his love for those who fear him; 12 as far as the east is from the west, so far has he removed our transgressions from us. 13 As a father has compassion on his children,

so the LORD has compassion on those who fear him; "NIV"

We also see that those who respect the LORD are blessed.

Ps 112:1

Blessed is the man who fears the LORD,

who finds great delight in his commands. "NIV"

Ps 31:19

19 How great is your goodness,

which you have stored up for those who fear you,

which you bestow in the sight of men

on those who take refuge in you. "NIV"

Ps 34:9

9 Fear the LORD, you his saints, for those who fear him lack nothing. "NIV"

Then we have God's promise and a warning to turn from evil.

Ps 34:11-16

11 Come, my children, listen to me; I will teach you the fear of the LORD. 12 Whoever of you loves life and desires to see many good days, 13 keep your tongue from evil and your lips from speaking lies. 14 Turn from evil and do good; seek peace and pursue it. 15 The eyes of the LORD are on the righteous and his ears are attentive to their cry; 16 the face of the LORD is against those who do evil, to cut off the memory of them from the earth. "NIV"

Ps 145:19-20

9 He fulfills the desires of those who fear him;

he hears their cry and saves them.

20 The LORD watches over all who love him,

but all the wicked he will destroy. "NIV"

In these passages, we see that God promised blessings to a select group. However, this was not necessarily for their benefit, it was to demonstrate to all of us who He is. God may accept anyone.

Ps 67:7

7 God will bless us, and all the ends of the earth will fear him. "NIV"

Acts 10:35

35 but accepts men from every nation who fear him and do what is right. "NIV"

This truth is the basis for understanding our relationship to God, or with Him. God is over us and He makes the rules. If we are to have a relationship with God, it must be on His terms. Whenever we disobey His rules, we deserve whatever punishment He deems appropriate. On the other hand, once we acknowledge that fact, we are open to having a relationship with Him.

God gives us the freedom to make choices.

You may have heard some say, "God is in control." While the Bible makes it very apparent that as creator of all, He can control anything He chooses to. However, the Bible is just as clear about God not controlling everything. Quite often, He just allows nature to take its course. He also allows us to make decisions that affect our lives and our relationship with Him.

The following reference list was produced from a search in the Bible for the phrase "if you will." If you take the time to look them up, you will find that God is declaring our free will to make choices. Sometimes the phrase "But if you," is an adjunct phrase. I believe it further emphasizes our free will, because He warns us of the consequences if we do not do as He has instructed us. These would come under the heading of conditional covenants as we looked at in the section on Judaism.

Gen 23:13, Gen 24:42, Gen 24:49, Gen 30:31, Gen 34:17, Gen 43:4, Gen 43:5, Lev 26:14, Num 21:2, Num 32:20, Num 32:20, Judg 6:36, Ruth 4:4, Ruth 4:4, 1 Sam 1:11, 2 Kings 5:17, 2 Chron 10:7, Job 5:1, Job 8:5, Jer 4:1, Jer 38:18, Zech 3:7, Matt 4:9

Some believe that since God is over all, that He controls every aspect of their lives. That He has a master plan in which we just play out our part and everything is predestined or foreordained. Even the days of our lives our numbered and you will die no matter where you are or what you are doing.

I first came across this concept serving as a medic in the infantry, in the jungles of Vietnam. Some guys just felt better believing that when it is your turn to die, it does not matter where you are. While this may make you feel better in a combat situation, it is illogical.

As I write this, I am reviewing the aftermath of Hurricane Katrina, which is one of, if not, the most devastating natural disasters to hit the United States. However, this pales in comparison to the Tsunamis in Asia when 230,000 were lost. Since then, we have had earthquakes in Pakistan killing an estimated 74,000 people. Added to this were floods and mudslides in China and India and hurricanes in Guatemala and El Salvador. It is hard for me to believe that God foreordained this. Rather, I believe that sometimes God just allows nature to take its course. After all, He created what we call nature. I believe God cares about us. As the Bible says, we are all precious in His sight. However, I believe he cares about how we live, not how long we live.

Others believe there is a balance between reward and punishment. Whatever we do, God will repay, kindness for kindness or evil for evil. Some call it karma, or what goes around comes around. However, anyone can see that life is not fair. Look at the words of Solomon, one of the wisest men who ever lived.

Eccl 9:11-12

11 Again I looked throughout the earth and saw that the swiftest person does not always win the race, nor the strongest man the battle, and that wise men are often poor, and skillful men are not necessarily famous; but it is all by chance, by happening to be at the right place at the right time. 12 A man never knows when he is going to run into bad luck. "TLB"

The consequences of our decisions are not always immediate.

Some people wonder why God lets bad things happen to good people. Of course, this question presupposes that God controls our lives, which He does not. Therefore, to gain a better perspective on this question, let us reverse it a bit. In the first place, if good was always rewarded, and evil always punished, we would be governed by this principle. It is like the carrot and the stick approach. When you do what God intends, you are rewarded, when you do not, you are hit with a stick. While that is true in general, every action we take does not have immediate consequences. Otherwise, there would not be a relationship of value to God. We would simply be responding to pleasure and pain.

In any of the above scenarios, God is over all, and we are subject to His will. However, consider this. If we were all just under His control, like puppets on a string, or characters in a play, what would be the point? For God, it would be like we were play toys. As such, we would certainly be meaningless to God.

On the other hand, what if God, who is all powerful, and

all knowing, decided to create us and give us the free will of whether to have a relationship with Him or not? Would not that relationship have more value to God, than if we had no choice? The fact is, He is still God, and can do whatever he wills. The value in the relationship comes when He gives us the free will to accept or reject Him.

God will judge us.

Throughout the Bible, God invites us to have a relationship with Him as a loving, forgiving father. On the other hand, if we reject Him as such, He will reject us. In either case, we are subject to His judgment.

Satan fools the majority of people by confusing them about God or leading them to believe there is no hell. He deceives many more about what we must do to enter heaven.

Satan would like you to believe:

▶ God sends you to hell for being bad.

▶ You earn your way to heaven by being good.

He wants us to take the focus off Jesus and put it upon ourselves.

However, the truth is:

▶ God admits you to heaven by accepting Jesus and placing your trust in Him.

▶ You send yourself to hell if you reject Jesus.

The choice is yours.

The Big Question.

If you were to die tonight, and found yourself standing before God, and He asked you, "Why should I let you into my heaven," what would you say?

Would it go something like this? "Well God, I think I have tried to be good. Maybe not perfect, but who is? I have taken care of my family. I never killed anybody. In fact, I was never in prison. I gave to some charities. I even volunteered to help others sometimes. I think that overall I have been fairly good."

Alternatively, if someone asked you what it takes to go to heaven and be with God, what would you tell him or her?

A common response is, "I don't know exactly. I guess, try to live your life the best you can. Be kind to others, don't cheat, or steal or things like that."

Your answer might be quite different if they told you that they had been informed two weeks ago that they only had three weeks to live. That would likely force you to focus more intently. However, for now, let us look at the more general response.

So by your standards, you think you will go to heaven, but what if God has different standards? What if God is Holy and pure, and does not allow anyone into heaven who is guilty of any sins at all? You might say, "That's impossible because nobody's perfect!" To which God might respond, "Actually, that is not quite true. One person did live a sinless life."

Yes, if it were up to us, nobody would be able to measure up to God's standard. That is why our loving God provides another way.

Two forms of judgment.

There are two forms of judgment mentioned in the Bible. One is for condemnation and the other for commendation. Either being found guilty of doing something wrong, or not doing what we should, results in condemnation and punishment. The opposite of that is a commendation that is awarded for doing what is right. For now, we will focus on the first form of judgment, which determines where you will spend eternity.

> *NT: 2922*
>
> *kriterion (kree-tay'-ree-on); neuter of a presumed derivative of NT: 2923; a rule of judging ("criterion"), i.e. (by implication) a tribunal:*
>
> *KJV - to judge, judgment (seat).*
>
> *(Biblesoft's New Exhaustive Strong's Numbers and Concordance with Expanded Greek-Hebrew Dictionary. Copyright (c) 1994, Biblesoft and International Bible Translators, Inc.)*

Picture yourself at a tribunal, which is like being the defendant in a court. Charges are read, accusations made, evidence displayed and the judge decides your guilt or innocence. If you are found guilty, they also decide the appropriate punishment.

At this point, you might be thinking, "No problem, I am not so bad. In fact I think I have been rather good." Lets' see how the prosecutor might accuse you based on some of the 10 commandments mentioned in the Bible.

"Your Honor, I accuse the defendant of violating your commandments:"

> *Ex 20:13-17*
>
> *13 "You shall not murder."*

> 14 *"You shall not commit adultery."*
>
> 15 *"You shall not steal."*
>
> 16 *"You shall not give false testimony against your neighbor."*
>
> 17 *"You shall not covet your neighbor's house. You shall not covet your neighbor's wife, or his manservant or maidservant, his ox or donkey, or anything that belongs to your neighbor." "NIV"*

You protest, "I never murdered anybody!" To which the prosecutor recalls the expanded meaning of this commandment by the words of Jesus.

> *1 John 3:15*
>
> *15 Anyone who hates his brother is a murderer, and you know that no murderer has eternal life in him. "NIV"*

You respond by defending yourself on the second charge. "But your honor, I never committed adultery!" To which the prosecutor quotes Jesus again:

> *Matt 5:28*
>
> *28 But I tell you that anyone who looks at a woman lustfully has already committed adultery with her in his heart. "NIV"*

"Ok, you got me there." You offer a weak excuse, "But I don't know of anyone who has never looked lustfully at someone." To that the judge says, "Guilty. What about the other charges?"

"Your honor, I never stole anything." To which the judge says, "Guilty as charged, and not only that, but you're also a liar too!"

Even if you are not convicted of your sin already, can anyone say they did not covet, or wished they had something that belonged to someone else?

In the end, you internalize that you have been found guilty of your sins so you switch tactics. "But your honor, look at all the good I have done!" To that, the prosecutor quotes scripture to complete his case against you.

> *Isa 64:6*
>
> *6 All of us have become like one who is unclean,*
>
> *and all our righteous acts are like filthy rags; "NIV"*

This does not mean that God does not care about the good things we do. In fact, He encourages us to do what is right. However, according to God's standards, our good deeds do not save us. They do not satisfy the requirements of the law to atone for our sins.

I believe there are two reasons for this. In the first place, many of the "righteous acts" people do are to gain recognition. If that is the motive, God is not impressed. He says we have already been rewarded. For example:

> *Matt 6:2-4*
>
> *2 "So when you give to the needy, do not announce it with trumpets, as the hypocrites do in the synagogues and on the streets, to be honored by men. I tell you the truth, they have received their reward in full. 3 But when you give to the needy, do not let your left hand know what your right hand is doing, 4 so that your giving may be in secret. Then your Father, who sees what is done in secret, will reward you. "NIV"*

The second reason is that your sins far outnumber your good

deeds. Let us say you just committed 3 sins a day. They do not have to be the big ones that they would put you in jail for. They could be something you have done, a sin of commission, or something you could have done but did not, a sin of omission. After a year, that would be about 1,000 sins, after 10 years, 10,000 sins and so on.

Does anyone really want to stand before God and try to argue that their good deeds outweigh their sins? If anyone thinks they are without sin, they are deceiving themselves.

1 John 1:8-10

8 If we claim to be without sin, we deceive ourselves and the truth is not in us. 9 If we confess our sins, he is faithful and just and will forgive us our sins and purify us from all unrighteousness. 10 If we claim we have not sinned, we make him out to be a liar and his word has no place in our lives. "NIV"

If you do not yet acknowledge that you are a sinner, according to God's standards, then you are probably lost and will spend eternity suffering in hell. As shown in the section for Jehovah's Witnesses, hell is real, and you do not want to go there. On the other hand, if you now begin to understand how you fall short of the perfection that God demands, then there is hope for you.

We can be saved from the judgment of condemnation.

The good news is that we can avoid this judgment.

John 5:24

24 "I tell you the truth, whoever hears my word and believes him who sent me has eternal life and will not be condemned; he has crossed over from death to life. "NIV"

The word for condemned in the original Greek implies a judgment that could result in damnation, or separation from God.

NT: 2920

krisis (kree'-sis); decision (subjectively or objectively, for or against); by extension, a tribunal; by implication, justice (especially, divine law):

KJV - accusation condemnation, damnation, judgment.

(Biblesoft's New Exhaustive Strong's Numbers and Concordance with Expanded Greek-Hebrew Dictionary. Copyright (c) 1994, Biblesoft and International Bible Translators, Inc.)

There is an illustration from the Bible to help us understand what God has done for us. As you read this, put yourself in the place of Joshua.

Zech 3:1-4

3:1 Then he showed me Joshua the high priest standing before the angel of the LORD, and Satan standing at his right side to accuse him. 2 The LORD said to Satan, "The LORD rebuke you, Satan! The LORD, who has chosen Jerusalem, rebuke you! Is not this man a burning stick snatched from the fire?"

Note that he was a burning stick, subject to judgment and damnation. Nevertheless, in God's mercy, he was rescued from the fire, or hell.

3 Now Joshua was dressed in filthy clothes as he stood before the angel. 4 The angel said to those who were standing before him, "Take off his filthy clothes."

Then he said to Joshua, "See, I have taken away your sin, and I will put rich garments on you." "NIV"

His clothes were made filthy by his sins, and Satan was standing ready to accuse him. However, God replaced his filthy rags with rich garments, symbolizing purity.

Zech 3:8-9

8 "'Listen, O high priest Joshua and your associates seated before you, who are men symbolic of things to come: I am going to bring my servant, the Branch.

9 See, the stone I have set in front of Joshua! There are seven eyes on that one stone, and I will engrave an inscription on it,' says the LORD Almighty, 'and I will remove the sin of this land in a single day. "NIV"

The *Branch* was a term used for Jesus the Christ, through whom God was going to atone for our sins, paving the way for a relationship with Him.

Understanding the relationship we can have with God.

Before we can have a relationship with God, we have to understand what makes us unacceptable. We are impure and cannot have a relationship with a holy God. It is not only by our actions, or how we appear outwardly. It is because our heart and mind is unclean before God.

Why do we appear unclean and unworthy to be with God?

In the Old Testament, God gave instructions about staying away from the things that make us unclean. For example, specific foods were to be avoided. Additionally, if we were exposed to certain things, we were considered defiled, or impure. However, this was not just for sanitary purposes to avoid disease. Some things were more symbolic to teach us about sin and its effect on us.

We all start as babies, innocent in the eyes of God. As we get older, we learn right from wrong. At some point, we reach an age where God will hold us accountable. He looks at our character, not just our actions.

This was what Jesus was referring to as he criticized the Pharisees. These religious leaders were teaching the people about observing the law in order to appear righteous, yet they were really unclean because their heart was not in the right place.

Matt 15:16-20

17 "Don't you see that whatever enters the mouth goes into the stomach and then out of the body? 18 But the things that come out of the mouth come from the heart, and these make a man 'unclean.' 19 For out of the heart come evil thoughts, murder, adultery, sexual immorality, theft, false testimony, slander. 20 These are what make a man 'unclean'; but eating with unwashed hands does not make him 'unclean.'" "NIV"

So, how do we become clean in the eyes of God?

It is not by attaining rightness with God after several lifetimes. Man's imagination has come up with the idea of reincarnation. Since nobody has ever lived a faultless life, it is nice to think we get a 2nd chance. In fact, why stop there? How about a 30th, or even a 100th chance to get it right? For some this concept has an appeal. Others, like Buddhists, would like to escape the struggles of life. However, as we have seen with Hinduism, it is not Biblical, nor is eternal progression as we saw with Mormonism.

The alternative is that we only get one lifetime to get it right. Either way, everyone can see that no one is perfect. Therefore, some conclude that God must judge us compared to other people. Otherwise, nobody would be acceptable to enter heaven. It is comforting to them to be able to look down at others and say, "Well, at least I am not as bad as that person." However, what if God's standards are perfection, not just being a little better than the next person?

There is a third option. We become clean in the eyes of God when our sins are forgiven, or when the requirements of the law have been satisfied. Think of this as though we owed a debt and either we repaid it or the person we owed the debt to forgave it and told us to consider it a gift.

God's way of accepting people.

That which is impure, must be purified. As an illustration, when refining gold, fire can be used to burn away the impurities. Maybe that gives us a glimpse of why a lake of fire is the final destination for the devil and those condemned to spending eternity suffering in hell. Fortunately, God provides another way.

Purification

In the Old Testament God prescribed methods of purification through ceremonial cleansing. When burnt offerings were made, salt was included. Since salt has both purifying and preserving properties, it was symbolic of Gods ability to cleanse us from our sins and preserve us too.

As we saw in the section on Roman Catholicism, without the shedding of blood there is no forgiveness for sin. This is why God instituted atonement for sins through animal sacrifice. As we saw in the section on Judaism, through the "Passover Lamb" and the scapegoat during "Yom Kippur" we could have our sins forgiven, by a substitute for our own blood. These animal sacrifices were inferior and had to be done repeatedly. They were symbolic of the atonement that was to come by Jesus as the Christ, or the "Anointed" one.

Heb 9:22-25

22 In fact, the law requires that nearly everything be cleansed with blood, and without the shedding of blood there is no forgiveness. 23 It was necessary, then, for the copies of the heavenly things to be purified with these sacrifices, but the heavenly things themselves with better sacrifices than these.

24 For Christ did not enter a man-made sanctuary that was only a copy of the true one; he entered heaven itself, now to appear for us in God's presence. 25 Nor did he enter heaven to offer himself again and again, the way the high priest enters the Most Holy Place every year with blood that is not his own. "NIV"

Atonement

Since sin makes us impure, one of the consequences is our separation from God. The atonement is God's way of cleansing us, in order to restore our relationship.

Atonement

The act by which God restores a relationship of harmony and unity between Himself and human beings. The word can be broken into three parts that express this great truth in simple but profound terms: "at-one-ment." Through God's atoning grace and forgiveness, we are reinstated to a relationship of at-one-ment with God, in spite of our sin.

(From Nelson's Illustrated Bible Dictionary, Copyright (c) 1986, Thomas Nelson Publishers)

We connect to God through Jesus. We who are impure rely on Jesus who is pure, to atone for our sins, bridging the gap between God and us. He, who was sinless, suffered the consequences of our sins, satisfying the requirements of a just and holy God.

Justification

Through the atonement of Jesus Christ, we are justified before God. To gain a better understanding of justification, think of it as "just-as-though-we-had-never-sinned." I like how the Living Bible expresses this:

Rom 3:21-25

21 But now God has shown us a different way to heaven --not by "being good enough" and trying to keep his laws, but by a new way (though not new, really, for the Scriptures told about it long ago). Now God says he will accept and acquit us-declare us "not guilty"-if we trust Jesus Christ to take away our sins. And we all can be saved in this same way, by coming to Christ, no matter who we are or what we have been like. 23 Yes, all have sinned; all fall short of God's glorious ideal; 24 yet now God declares us "not guilty" of offending him if we trust in Jesus Christ, who in his kindness freely takes away our sins.

25 For God sent Christ Jesus to take the punishment for our sins and to end all God's anger against us. "TLB"

Let us contemplate that. We can appear pure before God just as though we had never sinned. As such, God allows us to enter heaven and spend eternity with Him.

Adoption

There is only one Son of God. Nevertheless, Jesus said we could be adopted, with all the blessings of God, as His very own children.

Rom 8:15-17

15 And so we should not be like cringing, fearful slaves, but we should behave like God's very own children, adopted into the bosom of his family, and calling to him, "Father, Father." 16 For his Holy Spirit speaks to us deep in our hearts and tells us that we really are God's children. 17 And since we are his children, we will share his treasures-for all God gives to his Son Jesus is now ours too. "TLB"

Gal 4:4-7

God sent his Son, born of a woman, born under law, 5 to redeem those under law, that we might receive the full rights of sons. 6 Because you are sons, God sent the Spirit of his Son into our hearts, the Spirit who calls out, "Abba, Father." 7 So you are no longer a slave, but a son; and since you are a son, God has made you also an heir. "NIV

Sanctification

Even though through justification we appear before God as though we have never sinned, we did not become perfect, nor will we in this lifetime. Though we repent, and are no longer the slaves of sin, we face daily struggles. The Holy Spirit gives us the power to overcome temptation, but we still have our own free will, and sometimes we make poor choices. The good news is that we have help in our struggles. The Bible tells us that "sanctification" is the work of the Holy Spirit.

Sanctification

The process of God's grace by which the believer is separated from sin and becomes dedicated to God's righteousness. Accomplished by the Word of

God (John 17:7) and the Holy Spirit (Rom 8:3-4), sanctification results in holiness, or purification from the guilt and power of sin. (From Nelson's Illustrated Bible Dictionary, Copyright (c) 1986, Thomas Nelson Publishers)

God wants us to acknowledge that:

He is just and must punish *sin*, but He is also merciful and does not want to punish *us*.

Rom 6:23

23 For the wages of sin is death, but the gift of God is eternal life in Christ Jesus our Lord. "NIV"

He wants all to be saved.

God, our creator, loves each of us. It does not matter who you are, where you were born, your gender, the color of your hair or anything else. He knows that we have all sinned, made some poor decisions and have done some things we are not proud of. Yes, we are human and while God is righteous, holy, and pure, he loves us. That is why he provided a way to come to Him through a mediator.

1 Tim 2:3-5

3 This is good, and pleases God our Savior, 4 who wants all men to be saved and to come to a knowledge of the truth. 5 For there is one God and one mediator between God and men, the man Christ Jesus, "NIV"

However, not all will be saved; the choice is ours.

John 3:16

16 "For God so loved the world that he gave his one

and only Son, that whoever believes in him shall not perish but have eternal life. *"NIV"*

John 3:36

36 Whoever believes in the Son has eternal life, but whoever rejects the Son will not see life, for God's wrath remains on him." "NIV"

There is a great illustration for this. In an actual case decided by the United States Supreme Court, there was a person charged with a crime for which the penalty was death. He had been offered a pardon signed by the President. Instead of accepting it, he tore it up. The question arose, "Was the pardon valid if the person to be pardoned rejected it." The Supreme Court decided that if it was rejected, it was just as though no pardon was offered.

United States v. Wilson 32 U.S. 150 (1833)

"In the first United States Supreme Court case to be decided concerning the pardoning power, Chief Justice Marshall, speaking for the Court, said: A pardon is an act of grace, proceeding from the power entrusted with the execution of the laws, which exempts the individual, on whom it is bestowed, from the punishment the law inflicts for a crime he has committed. . ... A pardon is a deed, to the validity of which delivery is essential, and delivery is not complete without acceptance. It may then be rejected by the person to whom it is tendered; and if it be rejected, we have discovered no power in a court to force it on him."

Likewise, you have been offered a pardon, but if you reject it, you will suffer the consequences.

Salvation is free, and it frees us.

Salvation

The saving of man from the power and effects of sin.

Evangelical Dictionary of Theology. Copyright 1984 by Baker Books. All rights reserved. Used by permission.

Salvation is a free gift.

For it is by grace you have been saved, through faith- and this not from yourselves, it is the gift of God- not by works, so that no one can boast. Eph 2:8-9 "NIV"

As we saw in the section on Islam, grace is defined as, "Favor or kindness shown without regard to the worth or merit of the one who receives it and in spite of what that same person deserves." If someone offers you a gift, you have two choices. You can accept it or reject it. However, you cannot do something to pay or it, or it would no longer be a gift. If you reject it, it is though it was never even offered.

We are free from the consequences of sin.

It is critical that this sinks in. Do you fully understand and accept mercy versus guilt and punishment?

We are free from being a slave to sin.

Once cleansed from our unrighteousness by accepting Jesus, we receive the Holy Spirit who enables us to just say no. I am sure to many this seems like an oversimplification, but this is a promise from God.

1 Cor 10:13

13 No temptation has seized you except what is

common to man. And God is faithful; he will not let you be tempted beyond what you can bear. But when you are tempted, he will also provide a way out so that you can stand up under it. "NIV"

We are now free from our past, able to act like a different person, worthy of our new position.

Salvation involves more than believing in Jesus, it is trusting in him.

Just believing that Jesus existed is not enough. There is no doubt that he was an important historical figure. However, according to Ephesians 2:8,9 we are saved by faith. Salvation is dependent on placing your trust in Jesus. First, acknowledging that you are a sinner and deserving of punishment, then believing that Jesus was punished in your place. That he who was without sin, was punished as though he had sinned, in payment for your sins. Moreover, that it is Jesus alone, who lived a perfect, sinless, life who could satisfy the requirements of the law.

Acts 4:12

12 Salvation is found in no one else, for there is no other name under heaven given to men by which we must be saved." "NIV"

There is a great illustration about the difference between believing something and betting your life on it. As you read the following account, put yourself in the place of his manager.

Tightrope Walkers Jean Francois Gravelet, the great Blondin, was the first of many tightrope walkers to appear at Niagara Falls. He was a professional artist and showman trained in the great tradition of the European circus. At age 31 he came to America and made the announcement that he would cross the gorge of the Niagara River on a tightrope. On June 30, 1859, the rope was in position and at five o'clock in the afternoon Blondin started the trip that was to make history. Incredulous watchers saw him lower a rope to the Maid of the Mist, pull up a bottle and sit down while he refreshed himself. He began his ascent toward the Canadian shore, paused, steadied the balancing pole, and suddenly executed a back somersault. Never content merely to repeat his last performance, Blondin crossed his rope on a bicycle walked blindfolded, pushed a wheelbarrow, cooked an omelet in the centre and made the trip with his hands and feet manacled.

Yet even these stunts failed to satisfy Blondin's urge to test himself. He announced that on August 19 he would cross the gorge carrying his manager, Harry Colcord, on his back. It was to be the supreme test of Blondin's skill and stamina. According to Colcord, the trip was a nightmare. In the unguyed centre section, the pair swayed violently. Blondin was fighting for his life. He broke into a desperate run to reach the first guy rope. When he reached it and steadied himself, the guy broke. Once more the pair swayed alarmingly as Blondin again ran for the next guy. When they reached it Blondin gasped for Colcord to get down. Six times in all Colcord had to dismount while Blondin struggled to gather his strength. In the end Blondin had to charge the crowd on the brink to prevent the press of people forcing them back in the precipice. The Great Blondin had done it again, but this time he had only just made it. He died in England at the age of 73.

Source: The Niagara Parks Commission.

Now imagine yourself in the crowd cheering from the sidelines as he was performing. When he asked for a volunteer to be carried on his back as he traversed the falls, would you put your life in his hands?

Saving faith is like that. It is placing your full trust in Jesus Christ alone, not just cheering from the sidelines.

Salvation is by Jesus alone.

John 14:6

6 Jesus answered, "I am the way and the truth and the life. No one comes to the Father except through me. "NIV"

We are all guilty of sin and therefore warrant punishment. Jesus was sinless and not deserving of any punishment. If we suffer for our sins, that is justice. If he suffers in our place, we are offered mercy. The choice is ours. Either accept mercy and forgiveness, or be prepared to plead for your life, before a just and Holy God.

Decision time

Maybe by this point, you are ready to accept the pardon offered by God. You recognize that you are sinful and you do not want to be to be judged, rather, you want mercy. You now understand who Jesus is and are ready to put your trust in him. On the other hand, maybe your mind is closed and your heart is hardened.

There is a lesson to be learned from the parable of the sower. There is a warning here. Some people just never seem to understand, or their hearts are hardened. Others receive the word with joy, but it lasts only a short time. This demonstrates that if you are saved by faith, then you can also lose your salvation if you abandon your faith.

The warning and encouragement from the parable of the sower.

Matt 13:3-9

3 Then he told them many things in parables, saying: "A farmer went out to sow his seed. 4 As he was scattering the seed, some fell along the path, and the birds came and ate it up. 5 Some fell on rocky places, where it did not have much soil. It sprang up quickly because the soil was shallow. 6 But when the sun came up, the plants were scorched, and they withered because they had no root. 7 Other seed fell among thorns, which grew up and choked the plants. 8 Still other seed fell on good soil, where it produced a crop-a hundred, sixty or thirty times what was sown. 9 He who has ears, let him hear." "NIV"

Then Jesus explained the meaning.

Matt 13:18-23

18 "Listen then to what the parable of the sower means: 19 When anyone hears the message about the kingdom and does not understand it, the evil one comes and snatches away what was sown in his heart. This is the seed sown along the path. 20 The one who received the seed that fell on rocky places is the man who hears the word and at once receives it with joy. 21 But since he has no root, he lasts only a short time. When trouble or persecution comes because of the word, he quickly falls away. 22 The one who received the seed that fell among the thorns is the man who hears the word, but the worries of this life and the deceitfulness of wealth choke it, making it unfruitful. 23 But the one who received the seed that fell on good soil is the man who hears the word and understands it. He produces a crop, yielding a hundred, sixty or thirty times what was sown." "NIV"

There is also an encouragement. Some seed produced a crop. They shared their faith with others who became believers.

Would you like to know for sure, that if you died tonight, you would go to heaven?

In the previous section, we have placed an emphasis on trusting in who Jesus is, and what he has done for us. That is the foundation for salvation and eternal life. However, God expects more from us.

Are you willing to repent?

Have you come to the point where you not only confess your sins, but also are you willing to change your life?

Repentance

A turning away from sin, disobedience, or rebellion and a turning back to God (Matt 9:13; Luke 5:32). In a more general sense, repentance means a change of mind (Gen 6:6-7) or a feeling of remorse or regret for past conduct (Matt 27:3). True repentance is a "godly sorrow" for sin, an act of turning around and going in the opposite direction. This type of repentance leads to a fundamental change in a person's relationship to God.

(From Nelson's Illustrated Bible Dictionary, Copyright (c) 1986, Thomas Nelson Publishers)

Are you willing to obey?

Accepting the fact that Jesus is Lord is not the same as accepting him as your personal Lord and Savior. Are you willing to obey him?

Matt 7:21

21 "Not everyone who says to me, 'Lord, Lord,' will enter the kingdom of heaven, but only he who does the will of my Father who is in heaven. "NIV"

Luke 6:46

46 "Why do you call me, 'Lord, Lord,' and do not do what I say?" NIV"

John 14:15

15 *"If you love me, you will obey what I command.* "NIV"

As in one definition of disciple, illustrated in the section on Roman Catholicism, more than believing, it is adhering, or putting what they learned into practice. Here is another definition that is helpful to our understanding.

DISCIPLE

Disciple, Discipleship.

During Jesus' earthly ministry, and during the days of the early church, the term that was used most frequently to designate one of Jesus' followers was "disciple" (matheetees, 262 times). Hence, discipleship is a central theological theme of the Gospels and Acts. The situation is different in the Old Testament and in the rest of the New Testament. There is a curious scarcity of words for "disciple" in the Old Testament, and matheetees does not occur at all in the Epistles and Revelation. However, other terms and expressions point to abundant theological concepts of discipleship everywhere in Scripture. Discipleship enjoys its most concrete expression in Scripture when Jesus walked with his disciples during his earthly ministry. Yet, the Old Testament prepares for that relationship, and the Epistles and Revelation describe how that relationship was carried out after Jesus' ascension.

Called to a Relationship with God. The roots of biblical discipleship go deep into the fertile soil of God's calling. That calling is expressed in the pattern of divine initiative and human response that constitutes the heart of the biblical concept of covenant, manifested in the recurrent promise, "I will be your God, and you shall be my people." That call from Yahweh is reiterated in the call of Jesus, when he said, "Come to me, all you who are weary and burdened, and I will give you rest" (Matt 11:28). God has called his people to represent him on the earth, to be with him in every circumstance of life, to be transformed in personal character to be like him. That calling is at the heart of biblical discipleship, both in the Old and New Testaments.

Evangelical Dictionary of Biblical Theology. Copyright 1996 by Baker Books. All rights reserved. Used by permission.

As a side note, Yahweh, originally spelled YHVH, and pronounced Jehovah when translated from Hebrew to English, is the Jewish National name for God.

Are you willing to confess to others that Jesus is Lord?

Christians are in the minority. Jesus knew that confessing your belief in him would not always be the popular thing to do. Yet, he expects it from us. We are to be a light to the world, professing our faith in him.

Rom 10:9-10

9 That if you confess with your mouth, "Jesus is Lord," and believe in your heart that God raised him from the dead, you will be saved. 10 For it is with your heart that you believe and are justified, and it is with your mouth that you confess and are saved. "NIV"

Matt 10:32-33

32 "Therefore whoever confesses Me before men, him

> *I will also confess before My Father who is in heaven. 33 But whoever denies Me before men, him I will also deny before My Father who is in heaven. "NKJV"*

Friend, please do not let this concern you. God knows that in the beginning you are fearful of what others may think. Believe and trust the Holy Spirit, who will strengthen you. As you grow in your faith, nothing will be able to constrain you from declaring that Jesus is Lord!

This is the most important decision anyone makes.

Do not put off your decision. After death, it is too late. There is not a second chance.

> *Heb 9:27*
>
> *27 Just as man is destined to die once, and after that to face judgment, "NIV"*

It is your personal decision.

As you make your decision, remember that it has nothing to do with family, friends, or how or where you came to your current beliefs. It has everything to do with what Jesus has done for you. It is an invitation from God to accept mercy instead of justice.

It is *your personal* choice. We decide one at a time. It is not about your parents, your family, your friends, or any other outside influence. In fact, Jesus said we would be divided.

> *Matt 10:35-37*
>
> *35 For I have come to turn "'a man against his father, a daughter against her mother, a daughter-in-law against her mother-in-law- 36 a man's enemies will be the members of his own household.' 37 "Anyone who loves his father or mother more than me is not worthy*

of me; anyone who loves his son or daughter more than me is not worthy of me;" "NIV"

It is about how you respond to God. He is the one who offers the invitation. It does not matter what you would like to believe. It is not about your concept of God. It is all about God and what God wants, not you.

Your response to the invitation from God.

Speak to him in your words as a child would speak to their Father in heaven. Acknowledge that you have sinned and desire forgiveness. Let Him know that you desire a relationship with Him. He is waiting for you. An example prayer:

Father in heaven.

I acknowledge that you are holy and I am a sinner, unworthy of expecting anything from you but judgment, condemnation, and punishment. Nevertheless, I ask for your forgiveness and mercy.

I place my trust in Jesus, the Christ. I believe that he who was without sin, suffered and died in my place, so that I might appear sinless before you.

Jesus said that I can call you Father. That whoever places their trust in him can be adopted as one of your children. I ask that you accept me. I want to get to know you as my Father.

I want to spend eternity in heaven with you. Even now, I accept Jesus as both my Lord and Savior.

I pray for the gift of the Holy Spirit to help me live a life that would honor you.

I pray these things in Jesus' name, amen.

The Bible tells us that if you have just accepted Christ, the angels in heaven are rejoicing! God is waiting to help you as you begin your journey with Him.

After our decision, what is next?

You are born again.

"Born again?" What in the world does that mean?

John 3:1-8

3:1 Now there was a man of the Pharisees named Nicodemus, a member of the Jewish ruling council. 2 He came to Jesus at night and said, "Rabbi, we know you are a teacher who has come from God. For no one could perform the miraculous signs you are doing if God were not with him."

3 In reply Jesus declared, "I tell you the truth, no one can see the kingdom of God unless he is born again."

4 "How can a man be born when he is old?" Nicodemus asked. "Surely he cannot enter a second time into his mother's womb to be born!"

5 Jesus answered, "I tell you the truth, no one can enter the kingdom of God unless he is born of water and the Spirit. 6 Flesh gives birth to flesh, but the Spirit gives birth to spirit. 7 You should not be surprised at my saying, 'You must be born again.' 8 The wind blows

wherever it pleases. You hear its sound, but you cannot tell where it comes from or where it is going. So it is with everyone born of the Spirit." "NIV"

Born of the Spirit.

We are all born of the flesh, but we are not all born of the Spirit. To be born of the Spirit first means being dead to the flesh, or our earthly desires, then being open to guidance from the Holy Spirit.

Following Jesus in Baptism.

Jesus was baptized to fulfill all righteousness. The act itself symbolizes our death to the old nature, burial under the water, and resurrection as we come up out of the water. We are born again in the Spirit to live free from the bondage and penalty of sin.

Matt 3:13-15

13 Then Jesus went from Galilee to the Jordan River to be baptized there by John. 14 John did not want to do it.

"This isn't proper," he said. "I am the one who needs to be baptized by you."

15 But Jesus said, "Please do it, for I must do all that is right." So then John baptized him. "TLB"

In what is known as "The Great Commission," Jesus tells followers to baptize others.

Matt 28:18-20

18 Then Jesus came to them and said, "All authority in heaven and on earth has been given to me. 19 Therefore go and make disciples of all nations, baptizing them in the name of the Father and of the Son and of the Holy Spirit, 20 and teaching them to obey everything I have commanded you. "NIV"

John baptized with water for the repentance of sin.

The following verses from the Bible were after the resurrection of Jesus.

Acts 1:3-5

3 After his suffering, he showed himself to these men and gave many convincing proofs that he was alive. He appeared to them over a period of forty days and spoke about the kingdom of God. 4 On one occasion, while he was eating with them, he gave them this command: "Do not leave Jerusalem, but wait for the gift my Father promised, which you have heard me speak about. 5 For John baptized with water, but in a few days you will be baptized with the Holy Spirit." "NIV"

Note: the baptism Jesus was referring to was fulfilled at Pentecost.

We are to repent and be baptized in the name of Jesus Christ.

Note that Jesus was a common name. Baptizing in the *name of Jesus Christ* implies all the power and authority of the one and only Christ or anointed one. It is far more than just going through a ritual, as the following account illustrates.

Acts 19:1-6

19:1 While Apollos was at Corinth, Paul took the road through the interior and arrived at Ephesus. There he found some disciples 2 and asked them, "Did

> *you receive the Holy Spirit when you believed?" They answered, "No, we have not even heard that there is a Holy Spirit." 3 So Paul asked, "Then what baptism did you receive?" "John's baptism," they replied.*
>
> *4 Paul said, "John's baptism was a baptism of repentance. He told the people to believe in the one coming after him, that is, in Jesus." 5 On hearing this, they were baptized into the name of the Lord Jesus. 6 When Paul placed his hands on them, the Holy Spirit came on them, and they spoke in tongues and prophesied. NIV*

The power of the "name" of Jesus was also demonstrated in another passage where he was speaking of false prophets.

> *Matt 7:15-23*
>
> *15 "Watch out for false prophets. They come to you in sheep's clothing, but inwardly they are ferocious wolves. 16 By their fruit you will recognize them. Do people pick grapes from thornbushes, or figs from thistles? 17 Likewise every good tree bears good fruit, but a bad tree bears bad fruit. 18 A good tree cannot bear bad fruit, and a bad tree cannot bear good fruit. 19 Every tree that does not bear good fruit is cut down and thrown into the fire. 20 Thus, by their fruit you will recognize them.*
>
> *21 "Not everyone who says to me, 'Lord, Lord,' will enter the kingdom of heaven, but only he who does the will of my Father who is in heaven. 22 Many will say to me on that day, 'Lord, Lord, did we not prophesy in your name, and in your name drive out demons and perform many miracles?' 23 Then I will tell them plainly, 'I never knew you. Away from me, you evildoers!' "NIV"*

So you see, there are false prophets who use the name of Jesus knowing its power and authority, yet they do not really know him, therefore he denies them. It reminds me of when Jesus fed the 5,000 at one time and the 4,000 at another, with a few fish and loaves of bread. After this, some became followers of Jesus recognizing the miracles, while others just received a free lunch but nothing else. They missed the signs and wonders pointing to Jesus as the Son of God. In fact, there is another story in scripture about a magician who wanted to buy this power. He just did not understand that God was the source, and it was not for sale.

Infant baptism does not meet God's standard.

As noted in the section on Catholicism, throughout the Bible the emphasis is on the person being baptized, not the person baptizing them. We are to confess our sins, repent, and then be baptized. Nobody can do that for you. You cannot do that if you are a child under the age of accountability when you do not know right from wrong. So the question you need to answer is, have you been baptized since repenting and placing your trust in Christ?

Receiving the Holy Spirit

After Jesus was baptized, he received the Holy Spirit, as you can too.

> *Mark 1:9-12*
>
> *9 Then one day Jesus came from Nazareth in Galilee and was baptized by John there in the Jordan River. 10 The moment Jesus came up out of the water, he saw the heavens open and the Holy Spirit in the form of a dove descending on him, 11 and a voice from heaven said, "You are my beloved Son; you are my Delight."*

> *12 Immediately the Holy Spirit urged Jesus into the desert. There, for forty days, alone except for desert animals, he was subjected to Satan's temptations to sin. And afterwards the angels came and cared for him. "TLB"*

Jesus remained sinless, but the temptations were real. The Holy Spirit was with him to comfort and strengthen him. Likewise, the Holy Spirit can be our counselor and comforter.

We have the promise of receiving the gift of the Holy Spirit.

> *Acts 2:38*
>
> *38 Peter replied, "Repent and be baptized, every one of you, in the name of Jesus Christ for the forgiveness of your sins. And you will receive the gift of the Holy Spirit. "NIV"*

The Holy Spirit sanctifies us.

As noted earlier, the Bible tells us that "sanctification" is the work of the Holy Spirit. Those placing their trust in the atonement of Jesus appear *sinless* before a Holy God. Then, with the help of the Holy Spirit, we can *sin less*.

Let me give you an example of sanctification from my own experience. Earlier on, whenever I went to a restaurant and was given more change than I should have, I just looked at it as my lucky day. What I was really doing was cheating the server or owner out of their money. As I came to have an appreciation for God, I changed my perspective. I had a fear of God, which is the beginning of wisdom, and felt like God would get me for not being honest. I then progressed in my thinking to wanting to please God. I would point out the error to the server, but in a way, I was hoping that God would be pleased with me, because I was being honest. This was followed by my love of God, and my desire to please Him. In the end, my heart was changed to point out their error or return their money because I had learned to love them, as God would have me do.

Freedom from the consequences of sin does not make us free to sin.

Because Christ died for our sins, it does not mean we are free to live like the devil. Just after the resurrection of Christ, some were teaching that if you believed he paid the price for your sins you were free to do anything. In the following passages, Peter was addressing this false doctrine.

> *2 Peter 2:19-22*
>
> *19 "You aren't saved by being good," they say, "so you might as well be bad. Do what you like; be free."*
>
> *But these very teachers who offer this "freedom" from law are themselves slaves to sin and destruction. For a man is a slave to whatever controls him. 20 And when a person has escaped from the wicked ways of the world by learning about our Lord and Savior Jesus Christ, and then gets tangled up with sin and becomes its slave again, he is worse off than he was before. 21 It would be better if he had never known about Christ at all than to learn of him and then afterwards turn his back on the holy commandments that were given to him. 22 There is an old saying that "A dog comes back to what he has vomited, and a pig is washed only to come back and wallow in the mud again." That is the way it is with those who turn again to their sin. "TLB"*

What happens when we sin?

We are in rebellion to God. We may like to think that

whatever we do only affects us. However, most sin has a direct or indirect effect on others. Nevertheless, whenever we sin, we sin against God.

What happens if we sin after accepting Jesus as our savior?

We grieve the Holy Spirit. In chapters 4 and 5 of his letter to the Ephesians, Paul is emphasizing avoiding sin, no longer living as we once did, but now living as imitators of God, loving one another as God loves us. In verse 30, Paul implores us not to grieve the Holy Spirit, as though when we sin, it is not just involving ourselves, or someone we cause harm, but when we sin it pains God.

> *Eph 4:30-32*
>
> *30 And do not grieve the Holy Spirit of God, with whom you were sealed for the day of redemption. 31 Get rid of all bitterness, rage, and anger, brawling and slander, along with every form of malice. 32 Be kind and compassionate to one another, forgiving each other, just as in Christ God forgave you. "NIV"*

Note, that these are not big sins as some would think. We are not talking about rape and murder, but every kind of sin grieves the Holy Spirit.

What should we do when we sin?

Confess our sins to God. Acknowledge them, do not offer excuses, or ignore them. God wants you to be sincere. Recognize that all sin either hurts you, someone else, or causes separation from a Holy God. Therefore, it should make us feel sorrow.

Ask forgiveness. God is ready to forgive when you are genuinely sorry and ask to be forgiven. Repent. If you are sincere, it should be demonstrated by your desire to change your ways.

Can we lose our salvation by sinning?

The answer is illustrated in the following passage. In his letter to the Corinthians, Paul was scolding them for allowing someone who was openly sinning to remain among them as though nothing was wrong. God encourages us to flee from sin, not ignore it. This man was bringing down the others. Yet, even though Paul told them to remove this sinful person from their presence, note that his spirit would be saved.

> 1 Cor 5:1-5
>
> *5:1 It is actually reported that there is sexual immorality among you, and of a kind that does not occur even among pagans: A man has his father's wife. 2 And you are proud! Shouldn't you rather have been filled with grief and have put out of your fellowship the man who did this? 3 Even though I am not physically present, I am with you in spirit. And I have already passed judgment on the one who did this, just as if I were present. 4 When you are assembled in the name of our Lord Jesus and I am with you in spirit, and the power of our Lord Jesus is present, 5 hand this man over to Satan, so that the sinful nature may be destroyed and his spirit saved on the day of the Lord. "NIV"*

This passage reminds us that our faith is accounted to us for righteousness. Believers are justified before God to enter heaven based on the finished work of Jesus Christ. This illustrates that Jesus has done everything necessary to pass from judgment to eternal life. This is confirmed in the following passage, but it also reveals that God expects more from us.

> 1 Cor 3:12-15

> *12 If any man builds on this foundation using gold, silver, costly stones, wood, hay, or straw, 13 his work will be shown for what it is, because the Day will bring it to light. It will be revealed with fire, and the fire will test the quality of each man's work. 14 If what he has built survives, he will receive his reward. 15 If it is burned up, he will suffer loss; he himself will be saved, but only as one escaping through the flames. "NIV"*

Therefore, we are saved, but the fire will test our works. The bigger question is, "Have we lived the kind of life that God expects from us?" There is more on this later in this section.

We have an advocate.

Jesus is referred to here in his role as our advocate, or defense attorney. The word Satan is from the same Hebrew word that could be translated as accuser.

> *1 John 2:1*
>
> *2:1 My dear children, I write this to you so that you will not sin. But if anybody does sin, we have one who speaks to the Father in our defense-Jesus Christ, the Righteous One. "NIV"*

As we saw earlier in this section, Zech 3:1-4 gives us a picture from scripture regarding judgment and our advocate. The following is another illustration of the same point. Picture this:

We are standing before God, who is about to pass judgment on us. On one side, for the prosecution, we see Satan, the accuser. He tells God about all of our sins and why we should not be allowed into heaven. Then on the other side, we see Jesus, our advocate as our defense attorney. He pleads for us, not wanting any to perish.

For those who died acknowledging their sin, therefore deserving punishment, but placed their trust in Jesus, there is mercy. Believing that he had died in their place, already paying the price for their sins, they are justified before God, just as though they had never sinned. They have a righteousness that comes by faith.

Since we have forgiveness, does it matter if we sin?

Yes, being free from sin does not leave us free to sin.

Rom 6:15

15 Does this mean that now we can go ahead and sin and not worry about it? (For our salvation does not depend on keeping the law but on receiving God's grace!) Of course not! "TLB"

A few verses after explaining that the sacrifice of Jesus for the forgiveness of sins was done once for all, the author of Hebrews warns us.

Heb 10:26-27

26 If we deliberately keep on sinning after we have received the knowledge of the truth, no sacrifice for sins is left, 27 but only a fearful expectation of judgment and of raging fire that will consume the enemies of God. "NIV"

The Holy Spirit enables us to overcome sin.

Without God, we are on our own and slaves to sin. However, whatever addiction, with the help of the Holy Spirit, we can overcome anything.

1 John 4:4

4 You, dear children, are from God and have overcome

them, because the one who is in you is greater than the one who is in the world. "NIV"

The fruit of the Spirit.

We are promised blessings when we receive the Holy Spirit resulting in a changed life.

Gal 5:22-23

22 But the fruit of the Spirit is love, joy, peace, patience, kindness, goodness, faithfulness, 23 gentleness and self-control. "NIV"

The Spirit helps us with our daily problems.

He knows you better than you know yourself and He prays to the Father on your behalf.

Rom 8:26-28

26 And in the same way-by our faith --the Holy Spirit helps us with our daily problems and in our praying. For we don't even know what we should pray for nor how to pray as we should, but the Holy Spirit prays for us with such feeling that it cannot be expressed in words. 27 And the Father who knows all hearts knows, of course, what the Spirit is saying as he pleads for us in harmony with God's own will. 28 And we know that all that happens to us is working for our good if we love God and are fitting into his plans. "TLB"

Your true spiritual guide.

He will help you understand the scriptures.

John 14:25-26

25 "All this I have spoken while still with you. 26

But the Counselor, the Holy Spirit, whom the Father will send in my name, will teach you all things and will remind you of everything I have said to you. "NIV"

The Bible is the standard by which everything you hear must be measured.

Acts 17:11

11 Now the Bereans were of more noble character than the Thessalonians, for they received the message with great eagerness and examined the Scriptures every day to see if what Paul said was true. "NIV"

As we saw in the section on Mormons, it is important to read the verse before, the verse following, and in the context of the chapter, to gain the best understanding of any verse. Sometimes it is also necessary to view the chapter within the framework of the book, considering the author, to whom they were writing, and under what circumstances. Then view that within the standpoint of the Bible as a whole.

Reasons to meet with an assembly of believers.

There are many reasons to meet regularly with other believers, some for God, and some for us.

Worship

God alone is worthy of our worship and praise, and He expects it. Meeting with an assembly of believers promotes worship.

Neh 9:6

6 You alone are the LORD. You made the heavens, even the highest heavens, and all their starry host, the earth and all that is on it, the seas and all that is in them. You give life to everything, and the multitudes of heaven worship you. "NIV"

Ps 29:2

2 Ascribe to the LORD the glory due his name; worship the LORD in the splendor of his holiness. "NIV"

Ps 95:6-8

6 Come, let us bow down in worship, let us kneel before the LORD our Maker;

7 for he is our God and we are the people of his pasture, the flock under his care.

Today, if you hear his voice, 8 do not harden your hearts. "NIV"

Ps 96:9

9 Worship the LORD in the splendor of his holiness; tremble before him, all the earth. "NIV"

Ps 100:2-5

Worship the LORD with gladness; come before him with joyful songs. 3 Know that the LORD is God. It is he who made us, and we are his; we are his people, the sheep of his pasture.

4 Enter his gates with thanksgiving and his courts with praise; give thanks to him and praise his name. 5 For the LORD is good and his love endures forever; "NIV"

Communion

Jesus gave us symbols with which to remember him and what he did for us.

> *1 Cor 11:23-26*
>
> *The Lord Jesus, on the night he was betrayed, took bread, 24 and when he had given thanks, he broke it and said, "This is my body, which is for you; do this in remembrance of me." 25 In the same way, after supper he took the cup, saying, "This cup is the new covenant in my blood; do this, whenever you drink it, in remembrance of me." "NIV"*

Some churches observe communion once a week, some once a month, others only once a year. However, notice that Jesus said, "Whenever you drink it, do so in remembrance of me." It was not given as just some ritual to go through. It was given to us as a lasting reminder.

Spiritual Growth

In the following passages, Paul is chastising those who did not develop. They are still spiritual infants that have not grown. His scolding is both a warning and encouragement. Remember the parable of the seeds illustrated earlier.

> *1 Cor 3:2-3*
>
> *2 I gave you milk, not solid food, for you were not yet ready for it. Indeed, you are still not ready. 3 You are still worldly. For since there is jealousy and quarreling among you, are you not worldly? Are you not acting like mere men? "NIV"*

> *Heb 5:12-14*
>
> *12 In fact, though by this time you ought to be*

teachers, you need someone to teach you the elementary truths of God's word all over again. You need milk, not solid food! 13 Anyone who lives on milk, being still an infant, is not acquainted with the teaching about righteousness. 14 But solid food is for the mature, who by constant use have trained themselves to distinguish good from evil. "NIV"

Praying together

Praying for one another, also praying for those who have not yet believed, that they might be saved and come to a knowledge of the truth.

Matt 18:19-20

19 "Again, I tell you that if two of you on earth agree about anything you ask for, it will be done for you by my Father in heaven. 20 For where two or three come together in my name, there am I with them." "NIV"

Fellowship

Encouraging one another. Sometimes by sharing our experiences or our faith.

Heb 10:24-25

24 And let us consider how we may spur one another on toward love and good deeds. 25 Let us not give up meeting together, as some are in the habit of doing, but let us encourage one another-and all the more "NIV"

Your contribution to the body of believers.

God expects you to participate, not merely be an observer.

Rom 12:3-8

3 As God's messenger I give each of you God's warning: Be honest in your estimate of yourselves, measuring your value by how much faith God has given you. 4 Just as there are many parts to our bodies, so it is with Christ's body. We are all parts of it, and it takes every one of us to make it complete, for we each have different work to do. So we belong to each other, and each needs all the others.

6 God has given each of us the ability to do certain things well. So if God has given you the ability to prophesy, then prophesy whenever you can-as often as your faith is strong enough to receive a message from God. 7 If your gift is that of serving others, serve them well. If you are a teacher, do a good job of teaching. 8 If you are a preacher, see to it that your sermons are strong and helpful. If God has given you money, be generous in helping others with it. If God has given you administrative ability and put you in charge of the work of others, take the responsibility seriously. Those who offer comfort to the sorrowing should do so with Christian cheer. "TLB"

Eph 4:16

16 from whom the whole body, joined and knit together by what every joint supplies, according to the effective working by which every part does its share, causes growth of the body for the edifying of itself in love. "NKJV"

Collectively, we strengthen each other.

The Bible tells us that we all have certain God given talents. That does not mean that they are always developed or used as they should be. However, the Bible tells us that together we are much stronger than we are individually.

1 Cor 12:12-27

12 The body is a unit, though it is made up of many parts; and though all its parts are many, they form one body. So it is with Christ. 13 For we were all baptized by one Spirit into one body-whether Jews or Greeks, slave or free-and we were all given the one Spirit to drink.

14 Now the body is not made up of one part but of many. 15 If the foot should say, "Because I am not a hand, I do not belong to the body," it would not for that reason cease to be part of the body. 16 And if the ear should say, "Because I am not an eye, I do not belong to the body," it would not for that reason cease to be part of the body. 17 If the whole body were an eye, where would the sense of hearing be? If the whole body were an ear, where would the sense of smell be? 18 But in fact God has arranged the parts in the body, every one of them, just as he wanted them to be. 19 If they were all one part, where would the body be? 20 As it is, there are many parts, but one body.

21 The eye cannot say to the hand, "I don't need you!" And the head cannot say to the feet, "I don't need you!" 22 On the contrary, those parts of the body that seem to be weaker are indispensable, 23 and the parts that we think are less honorable we treat with special honor. And the parts that are unpresentable are treated with special modesty, 24 while our presentable parts need no special treatment. But God has combined the members of the body and has given greater honor to the parts that lacked it, 25 so that there should be no division in the body, but that its parts should have equal concern for each other. 26 If one part suffers, every part suffers with it; if one part is honored, every part rejoices with it.

27 Now you are the body of Christ, and each one of you is a part of it. "NIV"

God would like us to work together for the good of all.

Living a life that God rewards.

Doing good works does not save you. The constant theme of the Bible is that we cannot save ourselves; it is the gift of God. We are saved by grace through faith.

Rom 3:27-28

27 Then what can we boast about doing to earn our salvation? Nothing at all. Why? Because our acquittal is not based on our good deeds; it is based on what Christ has done and our faith in him. 28 So it is that we are saved by faith in Christ and not by the good things we do. "TLB"

However, just because you are saved, life does not end there. You are saved to do good works. Truly knowing Jesus should be evidenced in our lives. The following passage illustrates that we are encouraged to do things that have lasting value, like sharing the message of what Jesus has done for us with others.

> *Matt 6:20-21*
>
> *20 But store up for yourselves treasures in heaven, where moth and rust do not destroy, and where thieves do not break in and steal. 21 For where your treasure is, there your heart will be also. "NIV"*

Rewards and Punishment.

Earlier we discussed the two forms of judgment, one for condemnation, and the other for commendation. The good news, for those placing their trust in what Jesus Christ has done for them, is that they have passed the first judgment.

> *Rom 8:1-4*
>
> *8:1 Therefore, there is now no condemnation for those who are in Christ Jesus, 2 because through Christ Jesus the law of the Spirit of life set me free from the law of sin and death. 3 For what the law was powerless to do in that it was weakened by the sinful nature, God did by sending his own Son in the likeness of sinful man to be a sin offering. And so he condemned sin in sinful man, 4 in order that the righteous requirements of the law might be fully met in us, who do not live according to the sinful nature but according to the Spirit. "NIV"*

The bema judgment is for commendation. The nature of the judgment is clearly seen in the Greek word *bema* which is translated "judgment seat." In the Grecian games in Athens, the old arena contained a raised platform on which the person presiding would sit. From there, he rewarded all those who won crowns. It was a "bema," or rewarding seat. Likewise, as the word is used here, it tells us that those of us who have passed from the first judgment will be judged for how we live our lives. This is clearly illustrated in the following verses.

Matt 25:31-46

31 "When the Son of Man comes in his glory, and all the angels with him, he will sit on his throne in heavenly glory. 32 All the nations will be gathered before him, and he will separate the people one from another as a shepherd separates the sheep from the goats. 33 He will put the sheep on his right and the goats on his left. 34 "Then the King will say to those on his right, 'Come, you who are blessed by my Father; take your inheritance, the kingdom prepared for you since the creation of the world. 35 For I was hungry and you gave me something to eat, I was thirsty and you gave me something to drink, I was a stranger and you invited me in, 36 I needed clothes and you clothed me, I was sick and you looked after me, I was in prison and you came to visit me.'

37 "Then the righteous will answer him, 'Lord, when did we see you hungry and feed you, or thirsty and give you something to drink? 38 When did we see you a stranger and invite you in, or needing clothes and clothe you? 39 When did we see you sick or in prison and go to visit you?'

40 "The King will reply, 'I tell you the truth, whatever you did for one of the least of these brothers of mine, you did for me.'

41 "Then he will say to those on his left, 'Depart from me, you who are cursed, into the eternal fire prepared for the devil and his angels. 42 For I was hungry and you gave me nothing to eat, I was thirsty and you gave me nothing to drink, 43 I was a stranger and you did not invite me in, I needed clothes and you did not clothe me, I was sick and in prison and you did not look after me.'

> *44 "They also will answer, 'Lord, when did we see you hungry or thirsty or a stranger or needing clothes or sick or in prison, and did not help you?'*
>
> *45 "He will reply, 'I tell you the truth, whatever you did not do for one of the least of these, you did not do for me.'*
>
> *46 "Then they will go away to eternal punishment, but the righteous to eternal life." "NIV"*

This warning is for those who appear to have been saved yet are not. Otherwise, if they had a saving faith, it would be evidenced by their works.

> *James 2:14-18*
>
> *14 What good is it, my brothers, if a man claims to have faith but has no deeds? Can such faith save him? 15 Suppose a brother or sister is without clothes and daily food. 16 If one of you says to him, "Go, I wish you well; keep warm and well fed," but does nothing about his physical needs, what good is it? 17 In the same way, faith by itself, if it is not accompanied by action, is dead.*
>
> *18 But someone will say, "You have faith; I have deeds."*
>
> *Show me your faith without deeds, and I will show you my faith by what I do. "NIV"*

The Great Commission.

God expects more from us than being kind to one another. Several hundred years before Christ, God gave us stern instruction regarding our obligation to warn people who were in danger of judgment and need to repent.

> *Ezek 3:18-19*
>
> *18 When I say to a wicked man, 'You will surely die,' and you do not warn him or speak out to dissuade him from his evil ways in order to save his life, that wicked man will die for his sin, and I will hold you accountable for his blood. 19 But if you do warn the wicked man and he does not turn from his wickedness or from his evil ways, he will die for his sin; but you will have saved yourself. "NIV"*

After the resurrection, Jesus instructed us in what has become to be known as *The Great Commission.* If you also accept Jesus as Lord, you will do as he said.

> *Matt 28:19*
>
> *19 Therefore go and make disciples of all nations, baptizing them in the name of the Father and of the Son and of the Holy Spirit, "NIV"*

As we can see from the previous passage, God was speaking to all of us.

> *Matt 10:32-39*
>
> *32 "Whoever acknowledges me before men, I will*

> *also acknowledge him before my Father in heaven. 33 But whoever disowns me before men, I will disown him before my Father in heaven. 34 "Do not suppose that I have come to bring peace to the earth. I did not come to bring peace, but a sword. 35 For I have come to turn "'a man against his father, a daughter against her mother, a daughter-in-law against her mother-in-law- 36 a man's enemies will be the members of his own household.' 37 "Anyone who loves his father or mother more than me is not worthy of me; anyone who loves his son or daughter more than me is not worthy of me; 38 and anyone who does not take his cross and follow me is not worthy of me. 39 Whoever finds his life will lose it, and whoever loses his life for my sake will find it. "NIV"*

As for me, I know my home is in heaven. I am only here on temporary assignment. Whether here or hereafter, it makes no difference, Jesus is my Lord. That is why I had a burning desire to write this book.

How about you? Are you ready to obey Christ? Are you willing to share the good news of Jesus and offer salvation to others?

> *Luke 10:2*
>
> *2 He told them, "The harvest is plentiful, but the workers are few. Ask the Lord of the harvest, therefore, to send out workers into his harvest field. "NIV"*

Maybe you have friends or loved ones that you are concerned about. Maybe you have found it difficult to share your faith. Like so many, you have just tried to avoid arguments by not discussing anything as personal as religion. If so, my hope and prayer is that you will be able to reach others by sharing this book.

Resources

Bickel, Bruce and Jantz, Stan, *Bruce & Stan's Guide To The Bible*, Eugene, OR: Harvest House Publishers 1998

Bickel, Bruce and Jantz, Stan, *Bruce & Stan's Guide To Cults, Religions, And Spiritual Beliefs,* Eugene, OR: Harvest House Publishers 2002

Halverson, Dean C., General Editor, International Students, Inc. *The Compact Guide To World Religions*, Minneapolis, MN: Bethany House Publishers 1996

Ridenour, Fritz, *So What's The Difference?* Ventura, CA: Regal Books 1967, 1979, and 2001

Rhodes, Ron, *Find It Quick Handbook on Cults & New Religions*, Eugene, OR: Harvest House Publishers 2005

Muncaster, Ralph O., *Can You Trust the Bible?* Eugene, OR: Harvest House Publishers 2000

Muncaster, Ralph O., *How is Jesus Different from Other Religious Leaders?* Eugene, OR: Harvest House Publishers 2001

Goldmann, David, *Islam And The Bible,* Chicago, IL: Moody Publishers 2004

Rhodes, Ron, *Reasoning from the Scriptures with Muslims*, Eugene, OR: Harvest House Publishers 2002

Strobel, Lee, *The Case For Christ*, Grand Rapids, MI: Zondervan Publishing House 1998

Strobel, Lee, *The Case For Faith*, Grand Rapids, MI: Zondervan Publishing House 2000

Boa, Kenneth and Bowman, Robert, *20 Compelling Evidence That God Exists*, Tulsa, OK: RiverOak Publishing 2002

Ashton, John F., editor, *On the Seventh Day*, Green Forest, AR: Master Books 2002

Story, Dan, *Engaging the Closed Minded, Presenting Your Faith to the Confirmed Unbeliever*, Grand Rapids, MI: Kregel Publications 1999

Ankerberg, John and Weldon, John, *The Facts On The Roman Catholicism*, Eugene, OR: Harvest House Publishers 1993

Ankerberg, John and Weldon, John, *The Facts On Islam*, Eugene, OR: Harvest House Publishers 1991, 1998

Ankerberg, John and Weldon, John, *The Facts On The Mormon Church*, Eugene, OR: Harvest House Publishers 1991

Ankerberg, John and Weldon, John, *What Do Mormons Really Believe?* Formerly titled (and condensed from) *Behind the Mask of Mormonism*, Eugene, OR: Harvest House Publishers 2002

McKeever, Bill and Johnson, Eric, *Mormonism 101*, Grand Rapids, MI: Baker Books 2000

Reed, David A. and Farkas, John R., *How to Rescue Your Loved One from Mormonism*, Grand Rapids, MI: Baker Books 1994

Appendix A

The prophecies fulfilled in Jesus, the last days of his life.

1. Sacrificial lamb's bones not broken	Exodus 12:46	John 19:33-36
2. Body of cursed one hung on a tree shall not hang overnight	Deuteronomy 21:22,23	Luke 23:50-56 Galatians 3:13
3. Opposed by Kings and Rulers	Psalm 2:2	Mark 15:1
4. His forsaken cry	Psalm 22:1	Matthew 27:46
5. Onlookers mock and wag head	Psalm 22:6,7 Psalm 109:25	Matthew 27:39
6. Actual words of passersby	Psalm 22:8	Matthew 27:43
7. Hands and feet pierced	Psalm 22:16	Matthew 27:35
8. Stared upon	Psalm 22:17	Luke 23:35
9. Garments divided and gambled for	Psalm 22:18	John 19:24
10. Commits his spirit to God	Psalm 31:5	Luke 23:46

11. False witnesses rise up	Psalm 35:11	Mark 14:56
12. Friends stood afar off	Psalm 38:11	Luke 23:49
13. Betrayed by a friend who shared bread	Psalm 41:9	John 13:18-27
14. Suffered thirst	Psalm 69:21	John 19:28
15. Gall and vinegar offered	Psalm 69:21	Matthew 27:34
16. Rejected stone became cornerstone	Psalm 118:22	Matthew 21:42 Acts 4:10-12 1 Peter 2:6-8
17. Stricken on his back	Isaiah 50:6	Matthew 27:26
18. Spat upon	Isaiah 50:6	Matthew 26:67 Matthew 27:30
19. Appearance marred	Isaiah 52:14	Mark 14:65
20. Suffered for our sins	Isaiah 53:4,5,6,8,10,12	Romans 5:8,9 2 Corinthians 5:21 1 Peter 2:24

21. Dumb before accusers	Isaiah 53:7	Matthew 27:13,14
22. With rich man at death	Isaiah 53:9	Matthew 27:57-60
23. Numbered with transgressors	Isaiah 53:12	Mark 15:27 Luke 22:37
24. Interceded for sinners	Isaiah 53:12	Luke 23:34
25. Darkness at noon	Amos 8:9	Matthew 27:45
26. Sold for 30 Shekels of silver	Zechariah 11:12	Matthew 26:14,15
27. Silver thrown into the temple	Zechariah 11:13	Matthew 27:5
28. Pierced Body	Zechariah 12:10	John 19:34,37 Revelation 1:7
29. Shepherd struck; sheep scatter	Zechariah 13:7	Matthew 26:31

www.ingramcontent.com/pod-product-compliance
Lightning Source LLC
Chambersburg PA
CBHW071427070526
44578CB00001B/23